the best of home cooking

with **amy coleman**

the best of home cooking

with amy coleman

CHRONICLE BOOKS

SAN FRANCISCO

Questions about the show and recipes may be sent to:
Marjorie Poore Productions, 363 14th Avenue, San Francisco, CA 94118.

Library of Congress Cataloging-in-Publication Data:
The best of home cooking with Amy Coleman.
        p.   cm.
Includes index.
ISBN 0-8118-2256-7 (pbk.)
1. Cookery.   2. Home cooking with Amy Coleman (Television program)
I. Coleman, Amy, 1963–   II. Home cooking with Amy Coleman (Television program)
TX714.B425   1999
641.5—dc21   98-20860
CIP

Printed in Hong Kong.

Photographs by Darla Furlani.
Design by Kari Perin, Perin + Perin.
Typesetting by Words & Deeds.

10 9 8 7 6 5 4 3 2 1

Chronicle Books
85 Second Street
San Francisco, California 94105

www.chroniclebooks.com

Contents

Introduction

You're in the mood for some new ideas to *spruce up your recipe collection and decide to make a quick stop at your local bookstore to pick up a new cookbook. First you notice that the cookbook shelf now extends for several rows, or maybe has its own dedicated room. The choices are staggering. There are books on every topic, from dairy-free ice cream and sugarless desserts to Parmigiano and polenta. There are books for people who don't know the difference between a soufflé and cassoulet, and books for people who want details on the several hundred varieties of tomatoes that exist somewhere in the world. There are books small enough to carry in your pocketbook and others that require weight training. You quickly realize that the five minutes you allocated for this cookbook-buying venture are ridiculously short and you leave, either frustrated and bookless or very late for your next appointment.*

This scenario is just one of the inspirations *behind* Home Cooking, *a public television series that features a different cookbook and its author every week. The programs are a chance for viewers to watch cookbooks and their recipes come to life. It's an opportunity to meet the authors and creators of the books and actually watch them cook. It's a chance to hear great stories, lots of insider tips, and the kind of secrets that make the difference between ordinary cooking and great cooking.*

On both a personal level and as the *producer of the series, I have found* Home Cooking *to be an exciting source of new culinary ideas. We've had programs devoted to key cooking techniques like roasting, grilling, and baking, as well as hot food topics such as pizzas, salads, and pasta. We've included a great variety of ethnic cuisines, including Italian, Greek, Asian, Mexican, and French, and have devoted whole programs to special-interest books on smoothies, burgers, meatloaves, and pressure-cooking. We also*

brought in some of the best entertaining gurus in the country and picked their brains for their favorite recipes for parties and gatherings.

Each Home Cooking show is less than *half an hour, long enough to prepare only about three recipes. You may think that picking three recipes from one book with hundreds of choices would be difficult, but it's actually not. We always ask the authors if they have any favorites and, in almost every case, their eyes light up as they proceed to describe those one or two special recipes that always generate the most accolades and "oohs and aahs." Besides selecting author's favorites, we are very careful to pick recipes that do not have too many steps or hard-to-find ingredients. There's nothing worse than selecting a "quick" recipe that turns out to require half a day of ingredient shopping. We also like to include old-fashioned recipes with a new twist, like an interesting meatloaf, roast chicken, or biscuit recipe. To our surprise, these recipes always seem to inspire more than their share of viewer mail. We have also sought out recipes that are great for entertaining, since we know this is the time when people like to venture out and try new things.*

Every week, the Home Cooking shows *are viewed by millions of people who have different cooking skills. For some, cooking is a form of art; for many, it's a hobby; and for others, it can be a challenge. But there is one common thread that joins everyone—an appreciation of a delicious, home-cooked meal made with care and love. This book brings together a wonderful assortment of recipes that I believe will give home cooks at every skill level many hours of inspiration and enjoyment in the kitchen. I hope you'll try them and like them as much as we do.*

—Marjorie Poore, Producer

STARTERS

Rustic Ranch-Style Soup with Tomato, Jalapeño, and Avocado

RICK BAYLESS

3 quarts rich chicken broth
1 large head garlic, unpeeled
1 large sprig fresh epazote (optional)
2 fresh jalapeño peppers, stemmed
1 medium white onion, cut into
$1/4$-inch dice
2 large, ripe tomatoes, cored,
seeded, and cut into $1/4$-inch dice

Salt, about $11/2$ teaspoons, depending on
the saltiness of the broth
$3/4$ cup loosely packed chopped cilantro
About 1 cup coarsely shredded cooked
chicken (optional)
2 ripe avocados, peeled, pitted, and cut
into $1/2$-inch dice
1 lime, cut into 6 to 8 wedges

✳ Pour the chicken broth into a large pot. Slice the unpeeled head of garlic in half width-wise and add both halves to the broth along with the optional epazote. Bring to a boil, reduce heat to medium-low, and simmer, partially covered, for about an hour. The liquid should have reduced to about 7 cups (almost by half). Remove the garlic and epazote, and discard.

✳ While the broth is simmering, cut the peppers in half lengthwise, cut out the seed pods, and slice into very thin lengthwise strips. Set aside with the diced onion and tomatoes.

✳ Generously season the broth with salt, then add the peppers and onion, partially cover, and simmer for 7 minutes. Add the tomatoes, cilantro, and optional chicken and simmer for 3 minutes, then ladle into warm bowls. Garnish with avocados, serve to your guests, and pass the lime wedges separately for each person to squeeze in to their liking. *Makes 8 cups.*

VARIATION: Smoked chicken or other smoked poultry is delicious shredded into the soup. A little crème fraîche can be drizzled into the soup to make it richer.

SERVES 6 TO 8

IT IS BEST TO MAKE THIS SOUP WITH REALLY ripe, VINE-RIPENED TOMATOES. ONCE THE CONCENTRATED garlic FLAVOR HAS SWEETENED THE BROTH, THE SOUP IS ready IN A FLASH.

Tomato Bread Soup

1 tablespoon olive oil
6 cloves garlic, minced, plus ³/₄ teaspoon
 oil, or 3 teaspoons prepared minced
 garlic (see note)
1 teaspoon sugar
1 teaspoon chili powder
1 (14¹/₂-ounce) can diced tomatoes
1 (46-ounce) can tomato juice
Salt and freshly ground pepper
1 (15-ounce) can cannellini beans, rinsed
 and drained

Croutons
1 loaf Italian or French bread,
 cut diagonally into 18 slices
 approximately 1 inch thick
2 tablespoons olive oil
Garlic powder
¹/₂ cup freshly grated Parmesan cheese
Paprika
Cayenne pepper

1 cup loosely packed fresh basil leaves, cut
 into ¹/₈-inch-thick strips

✳ Heat the oil in a large stockpot over low heat. Add the garlic, sugar, and chili powder and sauté until aromatic, approximately 1 to 2 minutes. Add the tomatoes, tomato juice, salt, and pepper and simmer for 5 minutes. Just before serving, add the beans to the soup to warm through.

✳ To make the croutons, preheat the oven to 375°F and brush the bread slices with olive oil. Sprinkle each slice with some garlic powder, Parmesan cheese, paprika, and cayenne. Bake in the oven until golden brown, approximately 5 minutes. Cut each crouton in half.

✳ To serve, ladle the soup into 6 bowls. Place 6 crouton halves in the center of each bowl and garnish with the basil.

NOTE: To make prepared minced garlic, peel the cloves of 1 head of garlic. Mince in a food processor (do not purée) and add just enough olive oil to moisten the garlic and keep it from drying out. Transfer to a clean jar with a tight-fitting lid and store in the refrigerator for up to 1 week.

SERVES 6

THIS DELICIOUS SOUP WILL MAKE YOU forget ABOUT THE CANNED TOMATO SOUP OF YOUR childhood. IN FACT, WHEN SERVED WITH WHITE cannellini BEANS AND FRESH, CRISP CROUTONS, IT'S ELEGANT ENOUGH FOR A DINNER party. REMEMBER TO SLICE THE BREAD ON THE diagonal FOR AN ATTRACTIVE CROUTON.

Southwestern Corn Chowder with Chicken

SERVES 6

THE INCLUSION OF
potatoes IS WHAT
MAKES THIS ONE-POT
SOUP A chowder.
DREDGING THE CHICKEN
IN FLOUR BEFORE ADDING
IT TO THE SOUP ADDS FLA-
VOR AND GIVES THE SOUP
A THICKER, creamier
CONSISTENCY.

Flour, for dredging
1 1/2 pounds boneless and skinless chicken
    breast, cut diagonally into
    1/2-inch thick strips
2 1/2 tablespoons olive oil
1/4 teaspoon cayenne pepper
1 teaspoon chili powder
1/2 tablespoon dried oregano
4 cloves garlic, minced, plus 1/2 teaspoon
    oil, or 2 teaspoons prepared minced
    garlic (see page 13)
1 red onion, cut into 1/2-inch dice
1 Spanish onion, cut into 1/2-inch dice
2 red peppers, cut into 3/4-inch dice

1 jalapeño chili, minced
1 potato, peeled and cut into 1/2-inch dice
3 cups chicken stock (homemade or
    low-sodium canned)
1 (11-ounce) can corn, drained
    (or 1 1/4 cups frozen corn)
1 (15-ounce) can hominy, rinsed and
    drained
1 1/2 teaspoons salt, or to taste
2 limes, each cut into six wedges
    (optional)
1/4 cup scallions, green parts only,
    thinly sliced (optional)

✹ Place the flour in a large bowl. Dredge the chicken strips in the flour, shaking off any excess flour. Place a large pan over medium-high heat and allow the pan to heat up. Add 2 tablespoons of the oil, then add the chicken to the pan and sauté until golden brown.

✹ Remove the chicken from pan and set aside. Add the remaining ½ tablespoon oil, cayenne, chili powder, and oregano and toast over low heat for a few minutes to allow the flavors to be released. Add the garlic and sauté over medium heat until golden brown, approximately 1 to 2 minutes. Add the onions and peppers and continue to sauté until the onions turn golden, approximately 5 minutes. Add the potatoes and chicken stock and simmer for 5 minutes.

✹ Stir in the corn and the hominy and place the chicken on top of the soup. (Do not mix the chicken into the soup or it may overcook or get mushy.) Simmer over low heat for 10 minutes, or until the potatoes are tender. Add salt to taste.

✹ To serve, evenly distribute the chicken between 6 bowls and ladle the soup on top. Garnish with wedges of lime and sliced scallions, if desired.

Caramelized Onion Soup

LORA BRODY

Caramelized Onions

6 Vidalia onions (approximately 2¹/₂
    pounds; approximately 3 to 4 inches in
    diameter), stem and root ends sliced
    off, peeled, and left whole
¹/₂ cup (8 tablespoons) unsalted butter

Soup

3 to 4 cups caramelized onions *(from left)*
3 cups onion cooking liquid from
    the Crock-Pot
3 cups low- or no-salt vegetable,
    chicken, or beef broth
Salt and freshly ground pepper

✷ To make the caramelized onions, place the whole onions and butter in a Crock-Pot and cook on low until the onions are deep golden brown in color and very soft, anywhere from 12 to 24 hours. (Different Crock-Pots will take different amounts of time, but it is almost impossible to overcook the onions.) Set aside 3 to 4 cups for the soup and reserve the extra onions for another use (such as Sourdough Pizza with Potatoes and Caramelized Onions on page 85).

✷ To make the soup, combine the 3 to 4 cups caramelized onions, the onion cooking liquid, and the broth in a large pot, and warm over low heat until thoroughly heated. Season to taste with salt and pepper.

✷ To serve, evenly distribute the onions among 8 bowls and ladle the soup on top.

SERVES 8

CARAMELIZED ONIONS, slowly COOKED IN A CROCK-POT, ARE THE SECRET TO THIS rich SOUP CREATED BY LORA BRODY. YOU CAN easily SUBSTITUTE SPANISH OR EVEN REGULAR YELLOW onions FOR THE VIDALIAS. TO MAKE A nonfat VERSION OF THIS SOUP, ELIMINATE THE BUTTER AND COOK THE ONIONS IN ONE CUP OF BROTH.

Hunter-Style Mushroom Ragoût on Croutons

1 1/2 cups water
1 ounce dried shiitake mushrooms
1 ounce dried chanterelle mushrooms
1 ounce dried crimini mushrooms
1/2 tablespoon olive oil
4 garlic cloves, minced, plus 1/2 teaspoon oil, or 2 teaspoons prepared minced garlic (see page 13)
1 large onion, cut into large dice
1 1/2 cups fresh white button mushrooms, quartered
1/2 cup port wine
3/4 cup half-and-half

1 large tomato, peeled and cut into small dice
1 tablespoon lemon juice
Salt and freshly ground pepper

Croutons

1 loaf French bread, cut diagonally into 12 slices approximately 3/4 inch thick
1 tablespoon olive oil, or more as needed

1 1/2 tablespoons chopped fresh parsley, for garnish
1 1/2 tablespoons chopped fresh chives, for garnish

✱ Bring 1 1/2 cups water to a boil in a small saucepan. Add the dried mushrooms, remove from the heat, and let soak for 30 minutes. Strain the mushrooms and reserve the liquid.

✱ In large skillet, sauté the garlic in the olive oil over low heat until aromatic, approximately 1 to 2 minutes. Add the onion and sauté until translucent, approximately 3 to 5 minutes. Add the fresh and rehydrated mushrooms and sauté for another 2 minutes.

✱ Add the reserved mushroom soaking liquid and port to the skillet. Cook over medium-high heat until the liquid reduces in volume by one-half, approximately 6 to 8 minutes. Add the half-and-half, tomato, and lemon juice and bring to a simmer. Continue cooking until the mixture is thickened. Season with salt and pepper to taste.

✱ While the sauce is reducing, prepare the croutons. Preheat the oven to 375°F. Brush the bread slices with the oil and place on baking pan. Bake in oven until golden brown, approximately 12 minutes.

✱ To serve, spoon the mushroom ragoût into a serving bowl or onto individual plates and place the croutons alongside. Garnish with the parsley and chives.

SERVES 6

THIS earthy, RUSTIC STEW DERIVES ITS concentrated FLAVOR FROM THE COMBINATION OF wild AND DRIED MUSHROOMS. THE ragoût IS ALSO WONDERFUL SERVED ON TOP OF FILET MIGNON FOR A main COURSE.

Grilled Ratatouille

CHRIS JOHNSON

Basil Pesto
1/4 cup basil leaves
1/4 cup pine nuts
1/4 cup olive oil
2 cloves garlic, peeled
1 teaspoon lemon juice

Roasted Garlic
3 whole heads garlic
Olive oil
Salt and freshly ground black pepper

Reduced Balsamic Vinegar Sauce
1 1/2 cups balsamic vinegar

1 small eggplant, trimmed to 3 inches and
   cut into 1/4-inch slices
1 small zucchini, trimmed to 3 inches and
   cut into 1/4-inch slices
1 yellow bell pepper, cored, seeded, and
   cut into 6 wedges
1 red bell pepper, cored, seeded, and
   cut into 6 wedges
3 large Roma tomatoes, cut in half
Salt and freshly ground black pepper
6 tablespoons crumbled feta cheese

RATATOUILLE shaken up AND PUT BACK TOGETHER IN A WHOLE new WAY.

✻ To make pesto, place basil, pine nuts, olive oil, garlic, and lemon juice in a food processor or blender. Blend until smooth. Set aside.

✻ To make roasted garlic, preheat oven to 350°F. Cut off tops of heads of garlic. Drizzle tops of exposed garlic with a little olive oil and sprinkle with salt and pepper. Wrap in aluminum foil and bake for around 45 minutes. Remove from oven and when cool enough to handle, pop individual cloves from head. Set aside.

✻ To make reduced balsamic vinegar sauce, place vinegar in a medium saucepan and bring to a simmer. Simmer, uncovered, to reduce by two-thirds, about 1/2 hour. Set aside.

✻ Start a fire or turn gas grill to medium hot.

✻ Place eggplant, zucchini, peppers, and tomatoes in a large bowl. Season with salt and pepper and toss again. Place on a medium-hot fire and grill for 2 to 3 minutes per side. Remove from grill.

✻ On 6 individual serving plates, arrange the vegetables. Start with a slice of eggplant, followed by a red pepper wedge and another slice of eggplant. Follow with 2 pieces of zucchini and then a yellow pepper wedge. Top with a tomato half. (The vegetables are warm and can be gently pushed together.)

✻ Drizzle basil pesto over the vegetables and lightly over plate. Drizzle the plate with reduced balsamic vinegar sauce. Sprinkle with roasted garlic cloves and feta cheese and serve.

SERVES 6

Grilled Mozzarella with Tomato Vinegar

MICHAEL CHIARELLO

Tomato Vinegar
1 tablespoon olive oil
1 tablespoon minced garlic
1 cup peeled, seeded, and chopped vine-ripe tomatoes or good quality canned tomatoes
1/4 cup plus 1 cup water
4 ounces oil-packed sun-dried tomatoes, rehydrated in water
Salt and freshly ground pepper
1/2 cup champagne vinegar
2 tablespoons finely chopped fresh basil (optional)

4 very large romaine leaves
8 ounces fresh mozzarella cheese, cut into 4 equal pieces
Salt and freshly ground pepper
1 1/2 ounces dried prosciutto, diced
1 tablespoon extra-virgin olive oil
6 tablespoons tomato vinegar (see left), or more to taste
2 tablespoons Spanish or French extra-virgin olive oil
1 large bunch arugula, watercress, or other crisp, spicy green
2 tablespoons freshly grated Parmesan cheese

✴ To make the tomato vinegar, heat the oil in a small sauté pan over medium-high heat until almost smoking. Add garlic and sauté, moving the pan off and on the heat to regulate the temperature, until light brown. Add tomatoes and 1/4 cup water, and bring to a boil. Reduce heat to medium and simmer until thick. Add sun-dried tomatoes and cook until they soften, approximately 3 minutes. Season with salt and pepper. Purée tomato mixture in a blender. Add vinegar and thin with the remaining water, if necessary. Pulse in the basil, if desired. Adjust the seasoning with salt, pepper, and vinegar. Pour into a bowl or pitcher, then transfer to a clean, wide-mouth bottle or jar and cover with a nonmetallic lid. The tomato vinegar will keep in the refrigerator up to 1 week. *Makes 2 cups of tomato vinegar.*

✴ Bring a pot of salted water to a boil. Blanch the romaine leaves until they turn bright green and the central ribs are just tender enough to bend, approximately 30 seconds. Remove and immediately plunge the romaine into ice water to stop the cooking. Drain and pat dry.

✴ Prepare a grill or preheat the broiler. Lay the romaine leaves out on a clean work surface, rib-side down. Cut out the widest part of the central rib by making a triangular cut at the base of each leaf. Place a square of cheese in the middle of each leaf. Season with salt and pepper. Sprinkle each with approximately 1 tablespoon prosciutto. Make a neat package by folding the leaves around the cheese like an envelope, ending seam-side down. Brush each package with olive oil.

✳ In a bowl, combine the tomato vinegar and olive oil. Add the arugula or other greens and toss lightly to dress. Taste and add more vinegar, salt, and pepper, if necessary. Arrange the greens evenly in a wreathlike pattern on each of the 4 plates. Sprinkle the greens with some Parmesan.

✳ Place the cheese packages on the grill or put in a preheated broiler approximately 4 inches from the heat. Cook 2 to 3 minutes, then turn over. Cook for another 1 to 2 minutes, or just until the cheese begins to melt and the packages are soft to the touch and lightly brown. Do not let the cheese get too hot or it will toughen as it cools.

✳ To serve, set the grilled mozzarella in center of each salad plate. Serve immediately.

Nutty Pineapple Nibbles

6 celery stalks
1/4 cup canned crushed pineapple, drained
1/2 cup soft light cream cheese
2 tablespoons creamy peanut butter

1 tablespoon honey
1/4 cup raisins or dried fruit bits
1/4 teaspoon hot pepper sauce (optional)
3 tablespoons finely crushed dry-roasted nuts

✳ Rinse the celery, then trim off the leafy parts, and cut into 10-inch pieces.

✳ In a medium-sized bowl, combine the drained pineapple, cream cheese, peanut butter, and honey. Stir with a rubber spatula until well mixed. Stir in the raisins or fruit bits and hot sauce, if desired.

✳ Using a table knife, fill the groove of each celery stalk with the cheese mixture. Sprinkle the crushed nuts over the stalks.

SERVES 10

IT'S IMPORTANT TO GET kids INTO THE KITCHEN TO HELP THEM LEARN GOOD COOKING skills AND HEALTHY EATING HABITS. THESE AFTER-SCHOOL snacks ARE EASY AND FUN TO PREPARE. REPRINTED FROM *KID'S COOKBOOK* (AMERICAN HEART ASSOCIATION).

Bruschetta with Sweet Peppers and Ricotta

JANET FLETCHER

1 large red bell pepper
1 large golden bell pepper
¼ cup extra-virgin olive oil
1 large clove of garlic, minced
Salt and freshly ground black pepper

6 slices country-style bread, each about ¼ inch thick and 4 inches long
½ pound whole-milk ricotta cheese
6 to 8 fresh basil leaves, torn into small pieces

✳ Roast peppers over a gas flame or charcoal fire, or under a broiler, until blackened on all sides. Transfer to a plastic bag. Close the bag so that peppers steam as they cool. When cool enough to handle, peel the peppers, halve them, and remove the seeds. Cut peppers into strips ¼- to ½-inch wide.

✳ Heat 2 tablespoons of the olive oil in a skillet over medium heat. Add garlic and sauté until lightly colored, 1 to 2 minutes. Add peppers, season with salt and pepper to taste, and sauté until peppers are coated with oil and heated throughout. Remove from heat and cool in pan. For best flavor, sauté peppers 1 hour ahead so they can absorb the oil and exude their own juices.

✳ Toast the bread on both sides in a broiler, in a toaster oven, on a stove-top grill or—the best choice—over a charcoal fire. Remove from heat and drizzle one side of each slice with 1 teaspoon of olive oil.

✳ Season the ricotta cheese with salt and pepper and spread an even layer on each of the 6 toasts. Stir the basil into the peppers and divide the peppers and their juices among the 6 toasts. Serve hot.

Black Olive Tapenade

ROZANNE GOLD

2 cups pitted, oil-cured black olives
1 (2-ounce) can anchovies with capers,
   drained and patted dry

¹/₄ cup fruity olive oil
Freshly ground black pepper

✴ Put the olives and anchovies with capers in a food processor or blender. With the motor running, slowly add the oil until the tapenade is smooth; add an extra tablespoon of oil if necessary. Add freshly ground black pepper to taste.

Roasted Garlic and Bean Spread with Crusty Bread

JAMES MCNAIR

1 cup dried small white beans, such as
   cannelloni or flageolets, or 2 cups
   canned small white beans
2 or 3 whole heads garlic
Olive oil, preferably extra-virgin

Salt
Freshly ground black pepper
Fresh flat-leaf parsley for garnish
Sliced whole-grain French- or
   Italian-style bread

✴ If using dried beans, cook the beans according to the directions on page 100.

✴ To roast the garlic, preheat the oven to 350°F. Slice the heads horizontally, cutting away the top one-fourth to expose individual cloves. Peel away the outer papery skin, leaving the garlic heads intact. Place in a small baking dish, rub generously with olive oil, and sprinkle with salt. Cover tightly with aluminum foil and bake for 45 minutes. Uncover and roast until completely soft, about 15 minutes longer. Remove from the oven and set aside. When cool enough to handle, squeeze the garlic from the skin into a small bowl.

✴ Drain the beans and transfer 2 cups to a food processor or blender. (Cover and refrigerate or freeze any remaining beans for another purpose.) Add the roasted garlic and blend until fairly smooth. Season to taste with olive oil, salt, and pepper. Transfer to a small crock, garnish with parsley, and serve with sliced bread. *Makes 2 cups.*

Roasted Red Pepper Spread

BARBARA KAFKA

2 (7-ounce) jars roasted red peppers, drained
2 tablespoons extra-virgin olive oil
2 tablespoons minced fresh Italian parsley leaves

1 tablespoon fresh lemon juice
2 teaspoons capers, drained
1 medium clove garlic, smashed, peeled, and mashed to a paste with a pinch of salt

✻ Arrange the drained peppers on a double layer of paper towels and let them dry while preparing the recipe.

✻ Combine the remaining ingredients in the work bowl of a food processor. Process until the capers are very finely chopped. (This can also be done by hand with a chef's knife.) Add the drained peppers and pulse (or chop) until peppers are coarsely chopped. Stop several times to scrape down the sides of the work bowl to make sure the mixture is evenly chopped. Check the seasonings and adjust as necessary.

✻ Store the spread in a covered container in the refrigerator for up to 5 days. Remove to room temperature at least 30 minutes before serving.

MAKES 2 CUPS

THIS RECIPE IS easily MULTIPLIED USING JARRED RED PEPPERS AND WILL keep FOR UP TO 5 DAYS IN THE REFRIGERATOR. IT IS GOOD SERVED WITH VEGETABLE CRUDITÉS AND ON crostini.

Yogurt Sauce

MICHEL ROUX

2½ cups plain yogurt
½ cup mayonnaise
2 tablespoons snipped fresh herbs of your choice (such as chervil, parsley, chives, or tarragon)

1 medium tomato, peeled, seeded, and diced
Small pinch of cayenne (4 drops of hot pepper sauce can be substituted)
Salt to taste

✻ Mix all ingredients together. Sauce can be served at room temperature or chilled.

SERVES 8

THIS REFRESHING SAUCE IS excellent WITH ALL COLD VEGETABLES, COLD PASTA, FISH, and HARD-BOILED EGGS.

Smoked Salmon Napoleons

DENIS BLAIS

Pastry

4 sheets phyllo pastry

2 ounces clarified butter

2 tablespoons Parmesan cheese

2 tablespoons chopped fresh herbs (such as parsley, dill, tarragon, thyme)

1 cup radish sprouts, seeds cut off (mild arugula leaves can be substituted)

18 pieces smoked salmon (lox-style)

Extra chopped chives and drained capers for garnish

Dressing

1/2 cup buttermilk

1/4 cup sour cream

1/4 cup mayonnaise

1 teaspoon horseradish

Juice of 2 lemons

2 tablespoons finely minced chives

2 tablespoons capers, drained

Salt and freshly ground black pepper to taste

✽ To make the pastry, brush 1 phyllo sheet with butter. Lightly sprinkle with a little cheese and herbs. Repeat procedure with each sheet, stacking one on top of another.

✽ Preheat the oven to 300°F. With a small, sharp knife, cut phyllo dough into 4 x 6-inch pieces (for a total of 24), placing each on a large baking sheet. Place in oven and bake for 7 to 8 minutes, until golden. Remove from oven and allow to cool.

✽ While pastry is baking, combine all of the dressing ingredients in a bowl and whisk thoroughly. Set aside.

✽ To finish, place 1 cooled phyllo square in the center of a plate. Put a small bunch of radish sprouts on top of it, then a drop of dressing, then 1 folded slice of smoked salmon. Repeat 3 more times, alternating sprouts, dressing, and salmon. Top with another phyllo square. Assemble 3 more Napoleons per plate, and pour dressing onto the plate, surrounding the Napoleons. Garnish with extra chives and capers.

SERVES 6

CHEF DENIS BLAIS, ONE OF VANCOUVER'S premier CHEFS FROM THE MONTEREY BAR AND LOUNGE IN THE PACIFIC PALISADES HOTEL, picked THIS APPETIZER FOR BOTH ITS dazzling BEAUTY AND EASE OF PREPARATION.

Basic Cheese Quesadillas Several Ways

MARTHA ROSE SHULMAN

1 cup nonfat cottage cheese
1 1/2 ounces Monterey Jack, mild or sharp
   white Cheddar, or Parmesan cheese, or
   a combination, grated (approximately
   1/3 cup)

8 corn tortillas
Green or red salsa, for serving

✱ In a food processor fitted with the metal blade, blend together the cottage cheese and grated cheese until completely smooth.

✱ **To prepare the quesadillas using the oven,** preheat the oven to 400°F. Heat the tortillas one at a time, turning in a dry skillet over medium-high heat until flexible. Spread 2 tablespoons of the cheese mixture over each tortilla, leaving a 1/2-inch border around the edge, and fold the tortilla over. Place on an unoiled baking sheet. Heat, fill, and fold all the tortillas in this way. Heat through in the hot oven for 10 minutes, until the cheese melts and the tortillas just begin to crisp and curl up slightly on top. Transfer to plates and serve hot, passing salsa to spoon over the top.

✱ **To prepare the quesadillas using the stove top,** heat the tortillas, 2 or 3 at a time, in a dry skillet over medium-high heat until flexible. Spread 2 tablespoons of the cheese mixture over each tortilla, leaving a 1/2-inch border around the edge, and fold the tortilla over. Heat through, turning the folded tortilla over from time to time, until the cheese melts, approximately 5 to 8 minutes. Don't worry if some of the cheese runs out onto the pan (it probably will). Transfer to plates and serve hot, passing salsa to spoon over the top.

✱ **To prepare the quesadillas using the microwave,** wrap 4 tortillas in microwave-safe plastic wrap, a dampened towel, or wax paper and heat for 30 seconds to 1 minute in the microwave, until flexible. Spread 2 tablespoons of the cheese mixture over each tortilla, leaving a 1/2-inch border around the edge, and fold the tortilla over. Place on a plate or plates and cover with plastic, a paper towel, or wax paper. Repeat with the next 4 tortillas. Heat all the quesadillas through in the microwave for 2 minutes, uncover, and serve hot, passing salsa to spoon over the top.

Quesadillas with Goat Cheese, Roasted Peppers, and Black Beans

MARTHA ROSE SHULMAN

2 medium red bell peppers or pimientos
2 large garlic cloves, minced or pressed
2 ounces goat cheese, crumbled
    (approximately 1/2 cup)
3/4 cup nonfat cottage cheese
Salt and freshly ground pepper

2 cups cooked black beans in their
    cooking liquid, or 2 (15-ounce) cans
    black beans
8 corn tortillas
1 cup tomato salsa (homemade or
    prepared)

✳ To roast peppers, prepare a grill or preheat the broiler. Roast the peppers either directly over a gas flame or under a broiler, turning often until uniformly charred. When the peppers are blackened on all sides, transfer to a plastic bag, seal, and cool. Remove the charred skin, rinse, and pat dry. Remove the seeds and veins.

✳ In a food processor fitted with the metal blade, chop the garlic cloves. Add the roasted peppers (or pimientos) and process to a coarse purée. Add the goat cheese and cottage cheese and blend until smooth. Season with salt and pepper.

✳ Heat the beans in a saucepan over medium heat until simmering.

✳ Heat the tortillas, 1 or 2 at a time, in a dry skillet, following the instructions for the basic quesadillas on page 28. Transfer to plates and serve hot, passing salsa to spoon over the top.

SERVES 4

THREE DISTINCT savory FLAVORS MERGE HERE INTO A luscious, FILL-ING QUESADILLA. THESE taste SO RICH THAT YOU WON'T BELIEVE THEY'RE LOW IN FAT.

Black Bean Nachos

MARTHA ROSE SHULMAN

SERVES 12 TO 16

WHAT WE CALL *NACHOS* IN Tex-Mex COOKING ARE ACTUALLY CALLED *TOSTADOS* IN MEXICO: TOASTED tortilla CHIPS WITH A TOPPING. THERE ARE SEVERAL components TO THIS VERSION CREATED BY MARTHA ROSE SHULMAN, BUT THE REFRIED BEANS CAN BE prepared UP TO 3 DAYS IN ADVANCE AND KEPT IN THE REFRIGERATOR. THE *SALSA FRESCA* IS simple TO MAKE AND IS BEST PREPARED 15 MINUTES BEFORE SERVING.

Refried Black Beans

1 pound dried black beans or pintos, washed and picked over to remove any dirt or stones
1 onion, chopped
4 large garlic cloves, minced, or more to taste
2 to 3 teaspoons salt, or more to taste
2 large fresh epazote sprigs or 2 heaping tablespoons fresh cilantro leaves
2 tablespoons canola oil
1 tablespoon ground cumin
2 teaspoons pure ground mild or medium-hot chili powder

Salsa Fresca

1 to 1¼ pounds (4 medium or 2 large) tomatoes, finely chopped
½ small red onion, minced
2 to 3 jalapeño or serrano chilies, or more to taste (seeded and minced for a milder salsa)
¼ cup chopped fresh cilantro, or more to taste
1 to 2 teaspoons balsamic vinegar, rice wine vinegar, or fresh lime juice (optional)
½ teaspoon salt, or to taste

12 corn tortillas, cut into quarters or sixths

¼ pound *queso fresco, cotija,* or feta, crumbled, for garnish

✳ To make the refried beans, soak the beans in 6 cups water overnight, or for at least 6 hours. Drain the beans, then rinse with hot water and drain again.

✳ In a heavy-bottomed pot, combine the beans, onion, and 2 quarts fresh water, or enough to cover the beans by an inch. Bring to a boil, skim off any foam, and add 2 garlic cloves. Reduce the heat, cover, and simmer for 1 hour. Add the remaining garlic, the salt, and epazote, cover, and simmer for another hour, or until the beans are soft and their liquid is thick and soupy. Add salt to taste if necessary. Remove from heat.

✳ Drain the beans, reserving approximately 1 cup liquid. Mash half the beans coarsely in a food processor or with a bean or potato masher. (Do not purée them.) Stir the mashed beans back into the pot. Heat the oil in a large heavy nonstick skillet over medium heat and add the cumin and ground chili. Cook, stirring, over medium heat for about a minute, until the spices begin to sizzle and their pungent aromas are released. Raise the heat to medium-high and add the bean mixture. Fry the beans, stirring and mashing often, until they thicken and begin to get aromatic and crusty on the bottom. Stir up the crust each time it forms on the bottom of the pan and mix in with the beans. Cook for approximately 20 minutes, stirring often and mashing the beans with a bean masher or the back of a spoon. The beans should be thick but not dry. Add some of the reserved liquid if they seem too dry.

✳ Taste the refried beans and adjust the salt. Set aside in the pan if you're serving within a few hours. They will continue to dry out, so make sure you keep adding the remaining bean liquid. Otherwise, transfer the beans to a lightly oiled baking dish and cover with foil.

✳ Meanwhile, prepare the *salsa fresca:* Combine all the ingredients in a medium bowl and mix well. Let sit for at least 15 minutes before serving. (You should have 2 cups of salsa.)

✳ To toast the tortilla chips, preheat the oven to 325°F. Place the tortilla pieces on a baking sheet and bake for 20 to 30 minutes, until light brown and crisp, shaking the baking sheet every 10 minutes. Transfer to a rack to cool. Alternatively, to microwave the chips, place 6 to 20 pieces on a plate or on the plate in your microwave. Microwave on High for 1 minute. If the pieces are not crisp and are just beginning to brown, microwave for another 20 to 30 seconds, until crisp. Cool on a rack or in a basket.

✳ To serve the nachos, reheat the refried beans and spread a spoonful on each tortilla chip. Sprinkle on some cheese and dot with *salsa fresca*.

Beef Empanadas

BARBARA KAFKA

MAKES 48 EMPANADAS

A wonderful HORS

D'OEUVRE. PLAN TO

MAKE THE COMPONENTS

ahead SO YOU'RE NOT

SCRAMBLING WHEN YOUR

GUESTS arrive.

Empanada Dough

2¼ cups all-purpose flour

1 teaspoon kosher salt

6 tablespoons cold unsalted butter, cut into
    small pieces

2 eggs, lightly beaten

⅓ cup ice water

Beef Empanada Filling

2 teaspoons olive oil

¼ cup finely chopped onion

2 medium cloves garlic, smashed, peeled,
    and minced

2 teaspoons finely chopped fresh jalapeño
    pepper

½ pound ground beef

2 teaspoons kosher salt

1½ teaspoons ground cardamom

Freshly ground black pepper to taste

3 canned plum tomatoes, drained and
    roughly chopped

1 hard-boiled egg, finely chopped

2 tablespoons chopped fresh cilantro
    leaves

2 teaspoons fresh lime juice

Egg wash: 1 egg well beaten with a pinch
    of salt

✱ To make the dough, combine flour and salt in a large mixing bowl. Rub butter into flour mixture until it resembles coarse crumbs, or pulse in a food processor.

✱ Add the eggs and water and gently work the mixture together until it forms a ball; or pulse in a food processor until ingredients just combine into a loose ball. Remove dough from bowl or food processor and wrap in plastic wrap. Refrigerate for at least 2 hours.

✱ To make the filling, heat oil in a skillet over medium heat. Stir in the onion and garlic and cook for about 1 minute. Stir in the jalapeño and ground beef and cook, stirring, for about 5 minutes, or until meat has lost all pink color.

✱ Remove from heat and stir in remaining ingredients. Transfer to a bowl and allow mixture to cool completely before beginning to fill empanadas.

✱ Preheat oven to 350°F, placing a rack in the center of the oven. To fill empanadas, roll out dough on a lightly floured surface to about ¹⁄₁₆-inch thick. Cut out rounds with a 3-inch cookie cutter. Reroll scraps to use up all of the dough. Place 1 level teaspoon of filling in the center of each round. Lightly brush some egg wash halfway around the edge. Fold the pastry in half to form a turnover and pinch edges together to seal securely.

✱ Place empanadas on a baking sheet (not air-cushioned) lined with parchment paper. Brush tops of empanadas with egg wash and bake until golden brown, about 12 minutes. Remove from oven and allow to cool slightly before serving.

Chili Cheesecake

LORA BRODY

Butter for greasing pan
Corn chips to equal 1 1/2 cups of very
    fine crumbs
1/3 cup butter
2 pounds cream cheese at room tempera-
    ture (don't use whipped cream cheese)
1/3 cup heavy cream
4 extra-large eggs
2 teaspoons mild chili powder

1 or 2 chipotle (smoked jalapeño) peppers,
    minced (depending upon the desired
    heat)
1 cup smoked Gouda cheese,
    shredded or grated
1 medium onion, coarsely chopped and
    sautéed in 3 tablespoons butter
1/2 cup cilantro, finely chopped
1/3 cup very lean smoked ham, minced

✳ Preheat the oven to 300°F with the rack in the center position. Butter a 10-inch layer pan with 3-inch sides. Grind the corn chips in a food processor until very fine. Add the butter and pulse a couple of times. Use this mixture to coat the bottom and halfway up the sides of the pan.

✳ Place the cream cheese, cream, eggs, chili powder, and peppers into the food processor and process until completely mixed. Add the last 4 ingredients and pulse a few times to incorporate. (Do not process to a smooth consistency.)

✳ Pour the batter into the prepared pan, shake to level the top, and set the pan in a large roasting pan. Add hot water to a depth of 2 inches up the side of the cake pan.

✳ Place in oven and bake for 1 hour and 45 minutes. At the end of this time turn off the oven, but let the cake remain in the oven with the door closed for 1 more hour. Remove the pan to a counter and let rest for at least 1 hour more or until completely cool. Do not refrigerate.

MAKES ONE
10-INCH CAKE

THIS COMBINATION OF
smooth CREAM
CHEESE LACED WITH
THE ZING OF chili
MAKES FOR A NEW TAKE
ON A FIRST COURSE OR
appetizer. SERVE
WITH CRACKERS OR
STURDY TORTILLA CHIPS.

Gourmet Vegetable Turnovers

2 garlic cloves, minced, plus ¹/₄ teaspoon
   oil, or 1 teaspoon prepared minced
   garlic (see page 13)
1 tablespoon olive oil
1 medium (¹/₂ cup) onion, cut into
   small dice
¹/₂ large leek, white part only, halved
   lengthwise and sliced on the diagonal
   into ¹/₄-inch pieces (1 cup)
1 medium red pepper, cut into matchsticks

1 (15-ounce) can butter beans (or white
   kidney or cannellini), rinsed and
   drained
1 (14-ounce) can artichoke hearts, rinsed,
   drained, and quartered
¹/₄ teaspoon freshly ground pepper
3 ounces oil-cured olives, pitted and
   coarsely chopped
6 ounces goat cheese

1 box (2 sheets) puff pastry dough
1 egg, beaten

✱ In a large skillet, sauté the garlic over medium heat in the olive oil until golden, approximately 1 to 2 minutes. Add the onion and continue sautéing until translucent, approximately 3 to 4 minutes. Add the leek and pepper and sauté for an additional 3 minutes, or until the vegetables are softened but not mushy.

✱ Remove the pan from the heat. Add the beans, artichokes, and pepper and gently mix together. Turn the vegetable mixture out onto a baking sheet to cool. When cooled, transfer the vegetables to a large bowl and mix together with the olives and cheese.

✱ Preheat the oven to 400°F. Lightly grease a baking sheet.

✱ To assemble the turnovers, cover a large cutting board with plastic wrap, tucking the ends under the edges of the board. Cut each rectangular sheet of pastry in half, widthwise. Rewrap one of the halves for another use. Using a rolling pin, roll the pastry to less than ¹/₈-inch thickness. Cut each half vertically into 2 strips. You should have a total of 6 strips.

✱ Brush all the edges of the pastry well with the beaten egg. Evenly divide the filling into 6 portions and mound each portion onto the center of each pastry strip.

✱ Make a 1-inch slice into all four corners of each pastry piece. Fold both long flaps up, then fold the short side flaps, pinching the top corners to make a triangle. Brush the corners with the beaten egg to seal the edges.

✱ Place the filled turnovers on the baking sheet and bake for 25 minutes, or until the turnovers are golden brown. Serve immediately.

MAKES 6
TURNOVERS

THIS IS A wonderful FIRST COURSE FOR A DINNER party. YOU CAN MAKE THE VEGETABLES AHEAD AND USE STORE-BOUGHT puff PASTRY. WHEN YOUR GUESTS ARRIVE, SLIP THE turnovers INTO THE OVEN AND THEY'LL BE READY JUST IN TIME FOR DINNER.

SALADS

Shredded Chicken Salad with Spicy Sesame Vinaigrette

STEVEN WONG

Dressing

2 tablespoons honey

1 tablespoon Worcestershire sauce

1 1/2 cups Spicy Sesame Vinaigrette (see *below*)

2 cups bean sprouts (preferably mung bean)

2 tablespoons vegetable oil

3 cloves garlic, peeled and very thinly sliced lengthwise

1 pound Chinese-style steamed noodles or 8 ounces dried fettuccine

1 cup English cucumber, cut into thin matchsticks

1 cup carrots, cut into thin matchsticks

2 cups cooked chicken, beef, or pork, cut into julienne strips

1/2 cup thinly sliced green onions, green parts only

2 tablespoons sesame seeds

✱ In a small bowl or pot, combine all dressing ingredients and mix well. (If necessary, warm dressing over low heat or in a microwave to ensure honey is dissolved.)

✱ In a large bowl of ice water, refresh bean sprouts for 15 minutes until crisp. Drain and set aside.

✱ In a small skillet, heat oil over medium heat for 30 seconds. Add garlic and fry until light golden, about 2 minutes. (Be careful not to let it burn.) With a slotted spoon, remove garlic slices and discard. Reserve oil.

✱ In a large pot of boiling salted water, blanch noodles for 1 minute. Drain and, using chopsticks or two forks, toss to dry. (If using pasta, prepare according to package directions.) Transfer to a large salad bowl, toss with reserved garlic oil, and allow to cool.

✱ Add bean sprouts, cucumber, carrots, chicken, and green onions to noodles. Pour dressing evenly over salad; toss well. Sprinkle with sesame seeds and serve immediately.

Spicy Sesame Vinaigrette

1/2 cup soy sauce

1/2 cup Chinese red vinegar or balsamic vinegar

1 tablespoon sesame oil

1 tablespoon chili oil or 1 to 2 jalapeño peppers, thinly sliced

1 tablespoon minced fresh ginger

2 tablespoons water or chicken stock

✱ In a small bowl, combine all of the ingredients. Set aside for 30 minutes to develop flavors. Serve at room temperature. *Makes about 1 1/2 cups.*

SERVES 4

THIS IS A tasty WAY TO STRETCH LEFTOVER ROAST CHICKEN OR TURKEY. IN FACT, ROAST BEEF OR PORK WILL DO JUST AS well.

Roasted Root Vegetable Slaw with Gingered Apples, Raisins, Walnuts, and Barley

MARCEL DESAULNIERS

Gingered Apples, Raisins, and Walnuts
1/2 cup walnuts
1 cup port wine
1 teaspoon fresh lemon juice
1 Granny Smith apple, unpeeled
1 Red Delicious apple, unpeeled
1 tablespoon safflower oil
3/4 cup finely diced onion
1/4 cup finely diced celery
Salt and freshly ground black pepper
1/2 cup raisins
2 tablespoons cider vinegar
1 teaspoon grated fresh ginger

Brown Mustard Dressing
6 tablespoons spicy brown mustard
6 tablespoons pure apple juice
3 tablespoons mayonnaise
1 1/2 tablespoons cider vinegar
Salt and freshly ground black pepper

Root Vegetable Slaw
1 medium rutabaga, ends trimmed, peeled, and cut into strips 3 inches x 1/8 inch
2 medium carrots, ends trimmed, peeled, and cut into strips 2 inches x 1/8 inch
4 tablespoons safflower oil
Salt and freshly ground black pepper
2 small turnips, ends trimmed, peeled, and cut into strips 3 inches x 1/8 inch
2 medium parsnips, ends trimmed, peeled, and cut into strips 3 inches x 1/8 inch
1/2 cup Brown Mustard Dressing

Apple and Rosemary-Scented Barley
6 cups pure apple juice
1 teaspoon salt
1 teaspoon chopped fresh rosemary
1 1/2 cups pearl barley

1/2 pound washed and dried green leaf lettuce

✱ To make the gingered apples, raisins, and walnuts: Preheat the oven to 325°F. Toast the walnuts on a baking sheet in the oven for 10 minutes, or until lightly golden and fragrant, shaking pan occasionally. Cool the nuts and chop coarsely.

✱ Heat the port in a medium saucepan over medium-high heat. Bring to a boil, lower heat, and simmer, uncovered, for 15 minutes or until reduced to about 2 tablespoons. Remove from heat and set aside.

✱ In a nonreactive bowl, add the lemon juice to 2 quarts of cold water. Core and quarter the apples, then cut into 1/4-inch slices. Immediately place the apple slices in the water to prevent them from discoloring.

✱ Heat the 1 tablespoon of safflower oil in a large nonstick pan over medium heat. When oil is hot, add the onions and celery. Season with salt and pepper and cook, stirring, for 3 minutes.

✱ Drain the apples in a colander, rinse under cold water, and shake dry. Add to onion-celery mixture along with the raisins and the 2 tablespoons of cider vinegar and continue to cook, stirring occasionally, for 2 minutes. Add the ginger, stir to combine, and cook for 1 minute.

✳ Remove the pan from the heat, add the walnuts and port wine reduction. Stir to combine. Transfer to a nonreactive bowl and set aside, uncovered, at room temperature for up to 4 hours before serving. (Or cool to room temperature and refrigerate in a nonreactive, covered container for up to 4 days before serving.)

✳ To make the brown mustard dressing: In a nonreactive bowl, whisk together the mustard, 6 tablespoons of the apple juice, the mayonnaise, and the 1½ tablespoons cider vinegar until smooth. Adjust the seasonings with salt and pepper and whisk to combine. Cover tightly with plastic wrap and refrigerate until ready to serve. *Makes 1 cup.*

✳ To make the root vegetable slaw: Preheat the oven to 375°F. Place the rutabaga and carrot strips in a large, nonreactive bowl with 2 tablespoons of the safflower oil. Season to taste with the salt and pepper and stir to coat the vegetables with the oil. Transfer to a nonstick baking sheet. Spread out into a single layer covering the pan and set aside.

✳ Repeat the above process with the turnips and parsnips and place on a separate baking sheet.

✳ Place the baking sheets in the preheated oven. Roast the rutabagas and carrots for 10 minutes and the turnips and parsnips for 15 minutes. Cool the vegetables at room temperature for 30 minutes.

✳ Transfer the root vegetables to a large, nonreactive bowl, add ½ cup of the brown mustard dressing and use a rubber spatula to combine. Cover bowl tightly with plastic wrap and refrigerate for up to 2 days before serving.

✳ To make the apple and rosemary-scented barley: Heat the 6 cups of apple juice with 1 teaspoon of the salt and rosemary in a large saucepan over medium-high heat. When the juice boils, add the barley. Return to a boil, reduce to a simmer, and simmer for 45 minutes until barley is tender but not mushy.

✳ Drain the barley and then cool with cold water. Drain well and transfer barley to a large, nonreactive bowl. Cover tightly with plastic wrap and refrigerate for up to 2 days before serving.

✳ To assemble the salad: Divide and arrange the lettuce on 4 dinner plates. Arrange an equal amount of the barley on each plate, on top of the lettuce. Dress each plate with 2 tablespoons of the brown mustard dressing and place an equal amount of the root vegetable slaw in the middle of the barley on each plate. Portion an equal amount of gingered apples, raisins, and walnuts in the middle of the slaw on each plate. Serve immediately.

Vegetable Salad with
Crisp Sesame Seed Pancakes

SERVES 6

THE sesame PANCAKES PROVIDE A flavorful AND WONDERFUL PART-NER TO THIS VEGETABLE SALAD. THE secret INGREDIENT IN THE PANCAKES IS CREAM OF WHEAT™, WHICH MAKES A SURPRISINGLY DELICIOUS departure FROM YOUR EVERYDAY PANCAKE.

Sesame Pancakes
1 cup water
1/4 teaspoon kosher salt
3 tablespoons Cream of Wheat™ (not instant)
4 tablespoons sesame seeds
1/2 tablespoon olive oil

1 cup cauliflower florets
1 cup sugar snap peas
1 cup carrots, cut into large dice

1 cup broccoli florets
1 large red pepper, sliced into thin strips
2 tomatoes, peeled, seeded, and cut into large dice

Salad Dressing
3 tablespoons sesame oil
3 tablespoons rice wine vinegar
2 tablespoons honey
2 tablespoons Italian parsley, chopped
1 small bunch chives, thinly sliced
1/4 teaspoon fresh ground pepper

✳ To make the sesame pancakes, in a large saucepan, boil the water and salt. Whisk in the Cream of Wheat™ and 2 tablespoons of the sesame seeds. Boil for 3 minutes, stirring constantly.

✳ Line a small baking sheet with plastic wrap. Spoon the wheat mixture onto the baking sheet in 12 equal mounds. Cover with plastic wrap and pat each pile into a 1/3-inch thick pancake approximately 2 1/2 to 3 inches in diameter. Place the sheet in the refrigerator or freezer to cool.

✳ While the wheat mixture is cooling, blanch all the vegetables (except the tomatoes) separately in boiling water, each time cooking the vegetables until just al dente, then removing and running under cold water to stop the cooking.

✳ To make the salad dressing, place all ingredients in a food processor fitted with a metal blade or a blender and blend thoroughly.

✳ In a large bowl, toss the cooked vegetables and the tomatoes with the dressing and set aside.

✳ Remove the wheat patties from the refrigerator and dredge in the remaining 2 table-spoons sesame seeds to coat all over.

✳ In a hot nonstick pan over medium heat, sauté patties in olive oil until light golden brown on both sides, approximately 2 to 3 minutes on each side.

✳ To serve, place approximately 1 cup of the mixed vegetables on each plate and top with 2 pancakes.

Soothing Summer Turkey Salad

BARBARA KAFKA

1 cucumber, peeled, cut in half lengthwise, seeded, and cut crosswise into $1/4$-inch pieces

2 small tomatoes, cored and cut in $1/2$-inch cubes

$2^1/2$ teaspoons kosher salt

$3/4$ pound of 1-inch cubed roast turkey meat (about 2 cups)

2 scallions, trimmed and white and green parts cut into $1/2$-inch pieces

3 to 4 radishes, trimmed and sliced into very thin rounds

2 tablespoons chopped fresh dill

Freshly ground black pepper to taste

✱ Place cucumber and tomatoes in a medium bowl. Add salt and toss. Add the rest of the ingredients and toss gently. Let sit for 10 to 15 minutes at room temperature to allow flavors to develop. Serve on a bed of crisp lettuce greens.

Ditalini and Lentil Salad with
Smoked Salmon and Escarole

2 cloves garlic, minced, plus ¹/₄ teaspoon
    oil, or 1 teaspoon prepared minced
    garlic (see page 13)
¹/₂ tablespoon olive oil
2 carrots, cut into small dice
¹/₂ pound dried lentils
3 cups cool water
2 sprigs fresh thyme
1 bay leaf
¹/₂ cup (3 ounces) ditalini

1 tablespoon olive oil
¹/₄ cup red wine or sherry vinegar
3 plum tomatoes, diced (approximately
    ¹/₂ cup)
¹/₃ bunch scallions, green parts only,
    chopped (approximately ¹/₂ cup)
1 head escarole, Bibb lettuce, or
    Belgian endive, washed and dried
12 ounces smoked salmon, thinly sliced
    (approximately 18 slices)

SERVES 6

DITALINI ARE tiny, SHORT MACARONI. IF YOU CAN'T FIND IT, USE ANOTHER miniature PASTA, SUCH AS ORZO. THIS DISH MAKES A BEAUTIFUL PRESENTATION WHEN SERVED WITH smoked SALMON.

✳ In a medium-sized pot, sauté the garlic in the olive oil over medium heat for 1 to 2 minutes until golden. Add the carrots and cook for 2 to 3 minutes until they color slightly. Add the lentils, water, thyme, and bay leaf, and raise the heat to high. When the mixture comes to a boil, cover, reduce the heat, and gently simmer for approximately 25 minutes, or until the lentils are tender and most of the liquid has evaporated. (If the liquid evaporates before the lentils are tender, add additional liquid. Conversely, if they become tender but the mixture is still runny, drain the lentils.)

✳ In the meantime, while the lentils are simmering, cook the ditalini in boiling water according to the manufacturer's directions until al dente.

✳ Combine the cooked lentils with the pasta in a bowl and toss with the oil, vinegar, tomatoes, and scallions.

✳ To serve, fan the lettuce leaves on each plate. Evenly distribute the lentils in center of the plates, slightly covering the lettuce leaves. Drape 3 salmon slices over the lentils.

Grilled Caesar Salad

CHRIS JOHNSON

A CONTEMPORARY TAKE

ON THE CLASSIC CAESAR.

THE secret IS THE PRE-

SERVED LEMONS AND

FRIED CAPERS, WHICH

GIVE THE SALAD A

snappy ACCENT.

SERVES 6

Lemon Preserve

2 lemons, quartered, seeded, and each
     quarter cut into $1/8$-inch slices
4 cups water
$1/3$ cup sugar
$1/2$ cup white wine vinegar

Fried Capers and Caper Oil

1 cup canola oil
6 tablespoons medium capers, rinsed and
     patted dry

3 heads Romaine lettuce
$1^1/2$ cups of your favorite bottled Caesar
     dressing
2 cups toasted croutons
6 tablespoons grated Parmesan cheese

✳ To make lemon preserve, place lemon slices in a small saucepan with 2 cups of the water. Bring to a simmer and simmer for 20 minutes. Drain, and return lemon slices to saucepan. Add remaining 2 cups of water, sugar, and vinegar, and bring to a simmer, stirring to dissolve sugar. Simmer another 20 minutes, stirring often. Remove from heat and allow to cool.

✳ To make fried capers and caper oil, heat oil in a medium-size saucepan over medium-high heat. Add capers and cook until capers open. Remove capers with a slotted spoon and drain on paper towels. Set caper oil aside.

✳ Start a fire or turn gas grill to medium hot.

✳ Cut lettuce in half lengthwise, keeping stem intact, to create two open pieces held together by stem. Square off tops of lettuce pieces with a sharp knife. Place lettuce pieces, cut side down, over fire, and cook for about 2 minutes—the lettuce should be browned without turning black or burning. Turn and repeat on other side.

✳ Remove lettuce from grill and cut out connecting stem, creating 6 grilled pieces of lettuce. Place, cut side up, on serving plates.

✳ Drizzle 1 tablespoon of lemon preserve over each piece of lettuce, followed by 1 table-spoon of fried capers. Drizzle a teaspoon of caper oil over tops of salads. Drizzle about 4 tablespoons of Caesar dressing over each plate, followed by $1/3$ cup of croutons and 1 tablespoon of cheese, and serve.

Spicy Grilled Beef Salad

Spice Mix
1/2 teaspoon ground cumin
1/2 teaspoon curry powder
1/2 teaspoon garlic powder
1/8 teaspoon cayenne pepper

Dressing
1 cup chicken stock (homemade or low-sodium canned)
1 tablespoon cornstarch
1/4 cup peanut oil
1/4 cup cider vinegar, or wine vinegar
1/2 teaspoon sugar
1/2 teaspoon salt
1/4 teaspoon coarsely ground fresh pepper

1 1/2 pounds lean beef such as flank steak, beef tenderloin, or sirloin
Olive oil
Salt and freshly ground pepper
6 large handfuls mixed greens, such as radicchio, Belgian endive, and Boston Bibb, washed and well dried
12 scallions, white parts only, cut into 3-inch pieces
6 tomatoes, sliced horizontally 1/4 inch thick
1/4 cup roasted peanuts, toasted, for garnish (optional)
2 tablespoons chopped parsley, for garnish (optional)

✱ Preheat the oven to 325°F. To make the spice mix, combine the cumin, curry, garlic, and cayenne in small ovenproof sauté pan and toast in the oven for approximately 5 minutes until the spices release their aroma. (Alternatively, you can toast the spices on the stove top over low heat, taking care not to let them burn.) Set aside.

✱ To make the dressing, in a small saucepan, combine the chicken stock and cornstarch. Bring the mixture to a boil over medium-high heat. Lower the heat and simmer, whisking continuously, until the mixture thickens, approximately 1 to 2 minutes. Remove from the heat.

✱ In a medium bowl, whisk together the thickened stock, half of the toasted spice mix, the oil, vinegar, sugar, salt, and pepper. Set in the refrigerator if planning on serving a chilled salad, or leave hot for a warm salad.

✱ Rub the beef all over with the remaining half of the spice mix. Prepare a grill or preheat the broiler. Lightly brush the beef with oil, sprinkle with salt and pepper, and grill or broil to the desired doneness, approximately 2 to 3 minutes each side for rare to medium rare. Slice across the grain on a slight diagonal.

✷ To serve, place the greens in a mixing bowl and toss with just enough of the dressing to lightly coat the leaves. In a separate bowl, toss the the scallions and tomatoes with just enough dressing to coat. (Reserve and refrigerate any leftover dressing for another salad.)

✷ Divide the greens evenly among 6 plates and top with the scallions and a few tomato slices. Arrange the beef slices on top of the tomatoes and sprinkle the peanuts and chopped parsley all over, if desired, to garnish.

Cabbage Salad with Prosciutto

GEORGEANNE BRENNAN

2 1/2 cups shredded cabbage (a food
  processor fitted with a shredding disc
  works well)
1/4 cup extra-virgin olive oil
3 tablespoons red wine vinegar

1 tablespoon Dijon mustard
1/2 teaspoon salt
5 very thin slices prosciutto
1/2 teaspoon freshly ground black pepper

✷ In a large mixing bowl, toss together all of the ingredients except the black pepper. When well blended, stir in the pepper and remove to a serving bowl.

SERVES 3 TO 4

AN EXAMPLE OF simple INGREDIENTS COMBINED WITH A simple PREPARATION, CREATING A COMMANDING dish.

Green Bean Salad with Cherry Tomatoes and Ricotta Salata

JANET FLETCHER

Dressing

1/4 cup extra-virgin olive oil

1 tablespoon plus 2 teaspoons white wine vinegar

Salt and freshly ground black pepper

1/2 red onion, thinly sliced

Ice water

1 pound thin green beans (*haricots verts*), trimmed

1/2 pound small cherry tomatoes (preferably red and gold varieties mixed), halved

2 ounces ricotta salata cheese

✳ To make the dressing, whisk together olive oil, vinegar, and salt and pepper in a large bowl. (Beans need a lot of salt.) Whisk in onion and set dressing aside.

✳ Have ready a bowl of ice water. Bring a large pot of salted water to a boil over high heat. Add beans and cook until crisp-tender, about 5 minutes. Drain in a colander or sieve, then transfer beans to the ice water to stop cooking. When beans are cool, drain again and pat thoroughly dry with a clean dish towel.

✳ Add beans to bowl with dressing and toss to coat. Add tomatoes and toss again. With a cheese plane, shave the cheese directly into the bowl in paper-thin slices. Toss again gently to keep the flakes in large pieces, then transfer salad to a shallow serving platter.

SERVES 6

TENDER, SWEET, AND DELICATE, THE elegant GREEN FILET BEANS (ALSO KNOWN AS *HARICOTS VERTS*) DESERVE TO BE THE CENTERPIECE OF A summer MEAL. IF YOU CAN'T find RICOTTA SALATA—A SLICEABLE ITALIAN SHEEP'S MILK CHEESE—USE GREEK manouri OR ANY YOUNG SHEEP'S MILK CHEESE FIRM ENOUGH TO SHAVE INTO PALE flakes WITH A CHEESE PLANE.

Latin-Flavored Coleslaw with Grilled Avocados

CHRIS SCHLESINGER AND JOHN WILLOUGHBY

Dressing

3/4 cup mayonnaise
1/3 cup olive oil
1/3 cup fresh lime juice (about 2 large
   limes)
1/4 cup red wine vinegar
2 ears husked corn, blanched in boiling
   salted water for 2 minutes, drained,
   and kernels cut from cob (about 1 cup
   kernels)
2 tablespoons sugar
2 tablespoons catsup
4 to 10 dashes Tabasco sauce, to taste
Salt and freshly ground black pepper
   to taste

Coleslaw

2 cups shredded green cabbage
1 cup shredded red cabbage
1 cup shredded carrots (about 1 medium
   carrot)
3 ripe but firm avocados, halved and
   pitted, but not peeled
2 tablespoons olive oil
1 tablespoon chili powder
1 tablespoon ground cumin
Salt and freshly ground black pepper

* To make the dressing: In a food processor or blender, combine all the dressing ingredients and purée until smooth.

* To make the coleslaw: In a medium bowl, combine the green cabbage, red cabbage, and carrots. Add the dressing, mix well, cover, and refrigerate.

* Start a fire or turn gas grill to medium hot.

* Sprinkle the avocados with the olive oil, chili powder, cumin, and salt and pepper to taste. Place them on the grill over a medium-hot fire, cut side down, and cook for 3 to 5 minutes, or until seared. Pull the avocados off the grill and, as soon as they are cool enough to handle, turn them out of their skins, slice them, and serve them on top of generous helpings of the slaw. (If the avocados don't slip out of their skins easily, just spoon out chunks on top of the slaw.)

SERVES 4 TO 6

AIDED BY THE CHILI POWDER AND cumin, THE CUT SIDE OF THE AVOCADO SHOULD ACQUIRE A WELL-SEARED AND flavorful COATING. RIPE BUT FIRM IS THE ideal TEXTURE FOR THE AVOCADO, BUT YOU CAN GET AWAY WITH VERY FIRM OR MUSHY; anything BUT ROCK HARD.

BREAKFAST, BRUNCH, AND BREADS

Crazy Berries

MICHAEL CHIARELLO

Vanilla-Scented Sugar Syrup

4 cups sugar

1 cup water

2 vanilla beans, minced, or 2 teaspoons
  pure vanilla extract

Mango Vinegar

2 large, ripe mangoes, peeled and
  cut into ¹/₂-inch dice (approximately
  2¹/₂ cups)

¹/₂ cup vanilla-scented sugar syrup
  (from above)

Pinch of salt

¹/₂ cup champagne vinegar

2 cups fresh berries, such as raspberries,
  strawberries, or blueberries

¹/₂ cup superfine sugar

6 tablespoons mango vinegar
  (from left)

Pinch of salt and freshly ground pepper

Sweetened whipped cream or mascarpone
  cheese, for garnish (optional)

SERVES 6

THIS DESSERT IS CALLED

LAMPONE PAZZO IN ITALIAN.

YOU CAN USE WHATEVER

BERRIES ARE IN season.

USE A STORE-BOUGHT

MANGO- OR RASPBERRY-

INFUSED VINEGAR OR

MAKE your own

FOLLOWING THE DIREC-

TIONS INCLUDED HERE.

✳ To make the vanilla-scented sugar syrup, put the sugar, water, and vanilla beans, if using, in a pot and bring to a boil over high heat. Lower heat to a simmer and cook approximately 4 minutes. Stir occasionally. Let cool. Purée the syrup in a blender until vanilla beans are throughly chopped into the syrup. Strain through a fine strainer into a jar. If using vanilla extract instead of beans, add extract after the sugar syrup has cooled and pour into a jar. Seal tightly. *Makes approximately 3 ¼ cups.*

✳ To make the mango vinegar, purée the mangoes, ½ cup of the sugar syrup, and salt together in a blender. Add the vinegar and taste to balance. Add more vinegar and thin with water if necessary. Strain through a fine strainer into a bowl or pitcher. Store in a clean jar or bottle (do not use metal lids or tops) and refrigerate. *Makes approximately 2 ½ cups mango vinegar.*

✳ In a nonreactive bowl, combine the berries, sugar, mango vinegar, salt and pepper and set aside to marinate for 5 to 10 minutes.

✳ To serve, place the berries in individual bowls and garnish with a dollop of whipped cream or mascarpone, if desired.

Banana Latte Smoothie

MARY CORPENING BARBER, SARA CORPENING, AND LORI LYN NARLOCK

1 cup soy milk

$^3/_4$ cup strong-brewed coffee or espresso,
    room temperature or chilled

2 fresh bananas, frozen and sliced
    (see note)

6 to 8 ice cubes

1 teaspoon unsweetened cocoa powder,
    for garnish

$^1/_4$ teaspoon ground cinnamon, for garnish

✱ Combine the soy milk and coffee in a blender. Add the bananas. Blend until smooth. With the blender running, add ice cubes until they are incorporated and the desired consistency is reached. Pour into tall glasses and sprinkle with cocoa powder and cinnamon.

Classico Smoothie

MARY CORPENING BARBER, SARA CORPENING, AND LORI LYN NARLOCK

1 cup orange juice

1 cup hulled and quartered fresh
    strawberries, frozen

2 fresh bananas, frozen and sliced
    (see note)

✱ Pour the orange juice into a blender. Add the strawberries and bananas. Blend until smooth.

NOTE: To freeze bananas, peel, place in plastic bag, and freeze. Freeze several bananas at one time for quick use. Slice when ready to use.

Whole Wheat Pancakes with Blueberry Compote

MICHAEL NOBLE

Blueberry Compote

3 tablespoons sugar
1 tablespoon raspberry vinegar
1/4 cup orange juice
Zest from 1 orange, finely chopped
2 tablespoons port wine (optional)
2 cups (1 pound) fresh blueberries

Pancakes

1 cup all-purpose flour
1/2 cup whole wheat flour
3 teaspoons baking powder
1/2 teaspoon salt
3 tablespoons sugar
1 egg
3 tablespoons vegetable oil
1 1/2 cups milk, or more as needed
1/4 teaspoon vanilla extract

4 sprigs fresh mint, for garnish

SERVES 4

THIS IS ONE OF THE MOST popular BREAKFAST ITEMS AT VANCOUVER'S DIVA RESTAURANT. STAR CHEF MICHAEL NOBLE confesses THAT HE DID NOT INVENT THE RECIPE, BUT "BORROWED" IT FROM HIS mother. IF YOU CAN'T FIND FRESH BLUEBERRIES, SUBSTITUTE FROZEN BLUEBERRIES.

✴ To make the blueberry compote, place a small saucepan over medium heat. When the pan is medium hot, slowly add the sugar a sprinkle at a time while stirring constantly to melt. Continue cooking until the sugar turns to caramel.

✴ Pour in the raspberry vinegar and orange juice and deglaze the pan, scraping up the bits stuck to the pan. Add the zest and port, if desired, and continue to cook over medium heat until almost all the liquid has evaporated and the mixture starts to get thick and syrupy.

✴ Add the blueberries, bring to a simmer, and cook until the berries soften slightly, approximately 5 minutes. (If the compote is too runny, thicken it slightly with 1 teaspoon cornstarch dissolved in 2 teaspoons orange juice.) Serve warm.

✴ To make the pancakes, in a large bowl combine flours, baking powder, salt and sugar. In a separate bowl, whisk together the egg, oil, milk, and vanilla. Add the wet ingredients to the dry and mix to incorporate well. Let rest for 5 minutes.

✴ Pour 1/4 cup of batter onto a nonstick griddle or frying pan (do not add oil) and cook over medium heat. Cook until the edges of the pancakes are dry and small bubbles have formed on top, approximately 1 1/2 minutes; then flip with a spatula. Transfer to a 250°F oven to keep warm while repeating the procedure with the remaining batter.

✴ To serve, top the warm pancakes with 1/4 cup warm blueberry compote per person, and garnish with a sprig of fresh mint.

Breakfast Cobbler with Sausage, Apples, Onions, and Cheddar Cheese

1 pound breakfast sausage
3 medium onions, cut into large dice
3 medium-sized Golden Delicious apples,
   cut into large chunks

Cobbler Batter
2 teaspoons vegetable oil
$^1/_2$ cup sour cream, low-fat preferred
1 egg

$^1/_2$ cup yellow cornmeal
$^1/_2$ cup all-purpose flour
$^1/_2$ teaspoon baking powder
1 teaspoon baking soda
1 teaspoon salt
$^1/_2$ teaspoon freshly ground pepper
$^1/_2$ cup buttermilk

1 cup Cheddar cheese, grated

✳ Cut the sausage into large 1½-inch pieces. In large skillet, sauté the sausage over medium heat for approximately 10 minutes, until it begins to brown. Add the onions and apples to the pan and sauté until soft and golden, approximately 5 minutes, and set aside.

✳ To make the cobbler batter, place the oil, sour cream, and egg in a bowl and beat together with an electric mixer or by hand. In separate bowl, mix the dry ingredients together. Add the dry ingredients alternately with the buttermilk to the egg mixture until fully incorporated.

✳ Preheat the oven to 375°F. (If using a glass baking dish, bake at 350°F.) Grease a 9- x 12-inch baking dish and pour the filling mixture into the bottom of the dish. Evenly pour the batter on top of the filling and sprinkle with the cheese. Bake in the oven for 25 minutes, or until the top is golden brown and the batter is cooked through. (A toothpick inserted in the center should come out dry.)

✳ Let cool slightly before serving.

Vegetable and Chorizo Frittata with Tomato-Basil Chutney

MICHAEL NOBLE

Tomato-Basil Chutney

1/2 red onion, finely diced
1/2 red bell pepper, diced
1 teaspoon olive oil
3 tablespoons raspberry vinegar
1 tablespoon sugar
2 tomatoes, blanched, peeled, seeded and diced
2 teaspoons chopped fresh basil
Salt and freshly ground pepper

Frittata

1 potato, peeled, boiled until tender, and diced
4 tablespoons olive oil
1/2 medium onion, diced
1 red bell pepper, cut into thin strips
1 yellow bell pepper, cut into thin strips
8 ounces chorizo sausage, thinly sliced
2 cloves garlic, crushed or minced
12 eggs
6 ounces Monterey Jack cheese, grated
8 tablespoons tomato-basil chutney (see left), for garnish
4 sprigs fresh basil, for garnish

SERVES 4

THIS FRITTATA IS A star ATTRACTION AT THE world-famous DIVA RESTAURANT IN THE METROPOLITAN HOTEL IN VANCOUVER, B.C., AND COMES FROM THEIR EXECUTIVE CHEF AND CULINARY OLYMPIC winner, MICHAEL NOBLE. IF YOU'RE NOT PLANNING TO GO TO VANCOUVER, TRY THIS DISH, WHICH DOESN'T REQUIRE flipping, AT HOME.

✳ To make the tomato-basil chutney, in a medium saucepan, sauté the onion and the red pepper in olive oil over medium heat. Add the raspberry vinegar and sugar. Cook over medium heat until the liquid has reduced in volume by three-quarters, approximately 3 to 4 minutes. Add the tomatoes and cook 15 to 20 minutes, or until most of the liquid has evaporated. Add the basil and season to taste with salt and pepper. Keep at room temperature if serving right away or refrigerate overnight. *Makes 1 cup chutney.*

✳ To make the frittata, in a 12-inch nonstick frying pan, sauté the potatoes in 2 tablespoons of olive oil over medium heat until slightly brown, approximately 5 to 7 minutes. Add the onion and sauté for 2 minutes. Add the peppers, chorizo, and garlic and sauté for an additional 2 minutes, or until the onion and peppers become slightly browned. Remove from the pan and set aside.

✳ In a small bowl, beat 3 eggs. Heat an 8-inch nonstick frying pan over high heat with 1/2 tablespoon of the olive oil until lightly smoking. Add one-fourth of the vegetable and chorizo mixture and sauté for a minute or two. Pour the eggs over the mixture and stir vigorously with a spatula until the eggs start to set. Reduce the heat to low and let the eggs cook until the frittata comes loose from the sides of the pan when shaken.

✳ Preheat the broiler. Sprinkle the cheese over the top. Place frying pan in the broiler for a few minutes to firm up the top of the frittata. The frittata should slide easily out of the pan with the help of a spatula.

✳ Repeat the procedure for each of the 3 other frittatas. To serve, top each frittata with 2 tablespoons tomato-basil chutney and garnish with a fresh sprig of basil.

Meals in a Muffin

**MAKES 6
GIANT MUFFINS**

THESE oversized

MUFFINS, STUFFED WITH

SAVORY FILLINGS, ARE PER-

FECT FOR A packed

LUNCH OR A MIDDAY

snack. ADULTS WILL

APPRECIATE THE BOURSIN

AND HERB FILLING WHILE

KIDS WILL LOVE THE TRA-

DITIONAL FLAVORS OF

pizza. YOU CAN VARY

THE FILLING ACCORDING

TO YOUR taste.

3 eggs
¹/₄ cup oil
¹/₄ cup brown sugar
3 cups all-purpose flour
1 teaspoon salt
1 ¹/₂ teaspoons baking soda
2 cups buttermilk
1 teaspoon chopped fresh parsley
1 teaspoon chopped fresh chives

Boursin and Herb Filling
6 ounces Boursin cheese with garlic
³/₄ cup chopped scallions,
    green parts only
³/₄ cup chopped parsley

Tomato and Pepperoni Filling
³/₄ cup tomato sauce
3 ounces mozzarella cheese
3 ounces pepperoni

✳ In an electric mixer or using a hand mixer, beat the eggs, oil, and brown sugar together on low speed.

✳ In a separate bowl, mix together the flour, salt, and baking soda. Add the mixed dry ingredients alternately with the buttermilk and herbs to the egg mixture, and blend just until incorporated. (Do not overmix or it will toughen the batter.)

✳ Mix together the preferred filling ingredients.

✳ Preheat the oven to 375°F. Lightly grease a nonstick giant-size muffin tin (3½- x 1¾-inch) and fill each with ¼ cup of batter. (If you don't have a giant tin, the batter should fill 12 regular-size muffin tins.) Divide the preferred filling evenly among the muffin cups, approximately 3 ounces per muffin, then top each with an additional ¼ cup batter.

✳ Bake for 35 minutes, until the tops are golden brown and a toothpick inserted into the center comes out clean.

Cheese, Potato, and Rice
Galette with Smoked Ham

3 pounds Yukon Gold or Russet potatoes,
 peeled and quartered
6 ounces (approximately 4 1/2 cups)
 cooked wild rice mix (see *sidebar*)
3 ounces Gruyère or Swiss cheese, grated
3 ounces Parmesan cheese, grated
3 ounces smoked Gouda cheese, grated

6 ounces smoked ham, thinly sliced into
 1/2-inch squares
1/2 cup thinly sliced scallions, green parts
 only, or chives
1/2 teaspoon freshly ground pepper
2 tablespoons oil
Salmon caviar and sour cream,
 for garnish (optional)

✱ Fill a large pot with cold water, add the potatoes, and bring to boil. Drain right away (do not cook) and run under cold water to stop the cooking. Drain again and set aside to cool.

✱ When the potatoes are cool enough to handle, place in the bowl of an electric mixer fitted with a grating blade, and grate. Transfer the potatoes to a bowl and gently fold in the cooked wild rice mix, the cheeses, ham, scallions, and pepper.

✱ Preheat the oven to 375°F.

✱ Place an ovenproof, nonstick 13-inch skillet over medium-high heat, and let the pan get hot. Add the oil and then, using a wooden spoon, scrape the potato mixture into the skillet. Spread the batter evenly so that it creates a flat layer that reaches to the sides of the pan. Cook over medium-high heat for 8 to 10 minutes, or until the bottom of the galette is slightly browned. (If the galette begins to stick, shake the pan and scrape the batter off the bottom and reincorporate it into the mixture in order to form one solid pancake.) Place the skillet in the oven and finish cooking for 30 to 35 minutes, or until the bottom of the galette is golden brown.

✱ Run a long spatula underneath and around the sides of the galette to ensure that it is not stuck to the pan. Place a serving plate on top of the skillet and slowly flip the pan over, toward you.

✱ To serve, cut into 6 wedges and garnish each wedge with a dollop of sour cream and caviar, if desired.

SERVES 6

THIS galette IS ESPECIALLY EASY TO MAKE WHEN YOU HAVE left-over RICE. OTHERWISE, PREPARE A BOX OF WILD RICE mix ACCORDING TO THE MANUFACTURER'S INSTRUCTIONS. THERE IS NO NEED TO ADD SALT TO THE pancakes BECAUSE THE HAM AND CHEESES ARE QUITE SALTY. IF YOU DON'T HAVE A 13-INCH PAN, USE two 10-INCH PANS.

Neapolitan Ricotta, Mozzarella, and Prosciutto Pie

NICK MALGIERI

SERVES 8 TO 10

Dough

3 cups unbleached all-purpose flour

$^1/_2$ cup sugar

1 teaspoon salt

1 teaspoon baking powder

12 tablespoons (1$^1/_2$ sticks) cold unsalted butter

3 large eggs

Filling

2 pounds whole-milk or part-skim ricotta

6 large eggs

1 teaspoon freshly ground black pepper

$^1/_4$ cup grated Pecorino Romano cheese

1 pound mozzarella, coarsely grated

$^1/_2$ pound sweet dried sausage, peeled and diced

$^1/_2$ pound prosciutto, shredded

$^1/_2$ cup chopped fresh flat-leaf parsley

Egg wash: 1 egg well beaten with a pinch of salt

THE COMBINATION OF A sweet DOUGH AND A SALTY FILLING YIELDS A GOOD contrast— THE SWEETNESS OF THE DOUGH TEMPERS THE RATHER salty FILLING. IF THE COMBINATION DOES NOT APPEAL TO YOU, LEAVE OUT THE SUGAR; add A TABLESPOON OR TWO OF WATER TO MAKE THE DOUGH FORM A BALL.

✳ Butter an 11 x 17-inch jelly roll pan or a 12-inch-diameter x 2-inch-deep cake pan and set aside.

✳ To make the dough, combine the dry ingredients in the bowl of a food processor fitted with a metal blade and pulse several times to mix. Distribute the butter evenly over the dry ingredients in the work bowl. Pulse until very finely powdered. Add the eggs and continue to pulse until the dough forms into a ball on the blade.

✳ Remove the dough and divide into 2 pieces, one of which is two-thirds of the dough and the other one-third. Press the large piece into a circle and wrap in plastic. Press the smaller piece into a square and wrap in plastic, also. Refrigerate both pieces of dough while preparing the filling.

✳ To make the filling, place the ricotta in the work bowl of the food processor and pulse to purée until smooth. Transfer the ricotta to a mixing bowl and stir in the eggs, one at a time; stir in the remaining filling ingredients in the order listed.

✳ Set a rack at the lower third of the oven and preheat to 350°F.

✳ Lightly flour a work surface and the larger piece of dough and roll the dough into a 17-inch circle. Fold the dough into quarters and place in the prepared pan. Unfold the dough and press into the pan, allowing any excess dough to hang over the sides. Pour in the filling (it will come to about ¼ inch below the top of the pan) and smooth the top.

(continued on next page)

✳ Roll the remaining dough into a 10-inch square and cut into 1-inch strips. Paint the dough strips with the egg wash. Arrange 5 strips over the filling, leaving an even amount of space between strips. Arrange the remaining strips at a 45-degree angle across the first ones, creating a basketweave effect. Press the ends of the strips against the rim of the pan to make them stick and trim away excess dough—only from the strips—around the top of the pan. Use a small knife to loosen the bottom crust dough around the rim of the pan and fold it over to create an edge for the top crust.

✳ Bake the pie for about 45 minutes, until the filling is set and the dough is baked through. Don't overbake, or the filling will become watery and soak through the bottom crust. Remove from oven and cool in the pan on a rack.

✳ To unmold, place a platter over the pie and invert it, then remove the pan. Replace the pan with another platter and invert the pizza again. Remove the top platter.

✳ Keep the pie at room temperature the day it is baked. For longer storage, wrap in plastic wrap and refrigerate for up to several days. Bring back to room temperature before serving in small wedges.

New Orleans Bread Pudding with Southern Whiskey Sauce

3 tablespoons unsalted butter, softened
1 1/4 pounds French or Italian bread
   (1 1/2 to 2 loaves)
1 cup raisins
3 large eggs
4 cups whole milk

2 cups sugar
2 tablespoons vanilla
1 teaspoon ground cinnamon

Southern Whiskey Sauce (see below)

✱ Spread the butter on a 13 x 9-inch baking pan, preferably glass. Cut the bread into 1/2-inch slices. Arrange the slices almost upright in tightly spaced rows in the prepared pan. Tuck the raisins between the slices.

✱ Whisk the eggs in a large mixing bowl until frothy. Whisk in the milk, sugar, vanilla, and cinnamon. Pour mixture over the bread slices and let stand for 1 hour, pressing down now and then with a spatula to wet the tops of the slices.

✱ Preheat the oven to 375°F. Bake the pudding until the top is puffed and lightly browned, about 1 hour. Cover with Southern Whiskey Sauce and let stand on a rack for 30 to 60 minutes, then cut into squares and serve. Leftover sauced pudding will keep for several days in the refrigerator and can be reheated in a 300°F oven for 15 minutes.

Southern Whiskey Sauce

1/2 cup unsalted butter
1 cup sugar
1/4 cup bourbon or other whiskey
2 tablespoons water

1/4 teaspoon freshly grated or ground
   nutmeg
1/8 teaspoon salt
1 large egg

✱ In a small, heavy saucepan melt the butter over low heat. With a wooden spoon or heatproof rubber spatula, stir in the sugar, bourbon, water, nutmeg, and salt. Cook, stirring, until the sugar is dissolved and the mixture is blended. Remove from the heat.

✱ Whisk the egg until light and frothy. Vigorously whisk the egg into the liquor mixture. Set the sauce over medium heat and, stirring, bring to a simmer. Cook until thickened, about 1 minute. The sauce will not curdle. Serve at once, set aside at room temperature for 8 hours, or let cool, then cover and refrigerate for up to 3 days, reheating over low heat before using. *Makes 1 1/2 cups.*

SERVES 8 TO 12

THIS IS home COOKING AT ITS BEST. THE FINISHED DISH IS LIKE A warm STICKY BUN DRENCHED IN BUTTER AND BOURBON. THE SAUCE IS ALSO good WITH APPLE PUDDINGS OR ANY OTHER CAKE MADE WITH fruits OR NUTS. FOR A MILDER SAUCE, REPLACE HALF OF THE spirits WITH WATER.

Breakfast Pizza

BRENDA C. WARD AND JANE CABINESS JARREL

1 package refrigerated crescent rolls
1 pound reduced-fat turkey sausage
1 cup frozen shredded hash browns
1 cup reduced-fat Cheddar cheese, grated
5 eggs

1/4 cup skim milk
Reduced-fat Parmesan cheese
2 scallions, trimmed and cut thinly on the
   diagonal

✳ Preheat oven to 375°F. Unroll the crescent rolls and press together to form a solid crust in a 12-inch pizza pan.

✳ Brown the turkey sausage in a skillet. Remove the sausage and drain on paper towels. Crumble sausage over pizza crust.

✳ Sprinkle frozen hash browns over turkey sausage and top with cheese.

✳ Using a wire whisk, beat the eggs with the skim milk. Pour mixture over pizza.

✳ Sprinkle top of pizza with the Parmesan cheese and scallions. Place in oven and bake for 35 minutes or until set.

SERVES 6

THIS IS A HEARTY BREAK-FAST DISH FOR kids WHO WILL NOT ONLY HAVE A LOT OF fun PUTTING IT TOGETHER, BUT WILL enjoy ITS GREAT TASTE.

MAKES 2 LOAVES

BREAD MAKING IS easy
WHEN USING A STAND
MIXER, WHICH DOES ALL
OF THE WORK FOR YOU.
THIS wonderful
RECIPE IS FROM NARSAI
DAVID, SAN FRANCISCO'S
WIDELY loved FOOD
PERSONALITY.

Australian Flax and Sesame Bread

NARSAI DAVID

1/3 cup whole wheat berries
2 1/2 cups water
1 tablespoon active dry yeast
1 cup whole wheat flour
4 cups bread flour or all-purpose flour

2 tablespoons vegetable oil
2 tablespoons malt powder
1 1/2 teaspoons salt
1/3 cup flax seed, toasted
1/2 cup sesame seeds

✳ In a small saucepan, steam the wheat berries slowly with ½ cup of the water until the water is absorbed. Set aside to cool.

✳ Mix all ingredients except sesame seeds in a large mixing bowl and stir well. The dough can be kneaded either by hand or using a stand mixer with a dough hook.

✳ To make the bread by hand, turn dough out onto a floured surface and knead it until it is smooth and elastic, approximately 10 minutes. If using a stand mixer, knead the dough at low speed for 8 to 10 minutes.

✳ Place dough in a clean, large bowl. Cover with a kitchen towel. Set it in a warm, dry place to rise until dough has just about doubled in bulk, about 60 to 75 minutes.

✳ When the dough has doubled, turn it out onto a floured surface, punch it down, and divide it into 2 pieces. Form round loaves, taking time to round them up evenly until there are no wrinkles on top of the loaves. Moisten the loaves with a wet towel or a sprayer and roll in a bowl of sesame seeds.

✳ Place the loaves on a sheet pan dusted with flour or cornmeal (or onto a peel directly if you plan to bake on a baking stone). Cover loaves with a towel on the counter and let them rise until almost doubled, about one hour.

✳ With a razor blade, cut 4 deep gashes to form a very large square on the surface of each loaf. Cover again with the towel, and let the dough rise for another 10 to 15 minutes.

✳ While the loaves are rising, preheat the oven to 400°F with a rack positioned so that the bread will bake in the middle of the oven. If using a baking stone, it should be heating in the oven at the same time. Place the loaves in the oven and spray them well with a fine mist of water. Repeat the misting 2 more times at 10-minute intervals. Bake for about 45 minutes until a nice firm crust has formed. Test the doneness by rapping the bottom with your knuckle. The loaf should be firm and make a hollow sound. Cool on a wire rack.

Touch of Grace Biscuits

SHIRLEY CORRIHER

Nonstick cooking spray
1 1/2 cups Southern self-rising flour (*see note*)
1/8 teaspoon baking soda
1/3 teaspoon salt
1 tablespoon sugar
3 tablespoons shortening

1 to 1 1/4 cups buttermilk or 3/4 cup buttermilk and 1/2 cup heavy cream
1 cup bleached all-purpose flour for shaping dough
2 tablespoons butter, melted

✳ Preheat the oven to 475°F and spray an 8-inch round cake pan with nonstick cooking spray.

✳ In a medium mixing bowl, combine the flour, soda, salt, and sugar. With your fingers or a pastry cutter, work the shortening into the flour mixture until there are no shortening lumps larger than a big pea.

✳ Stir in the buttermilk and let stand for 2 to 3 minutes. This dough is so wet you cannot shape it in the usual manner.

✳ Pour the cup of all-purpose flour onto a plate or pie tin. Flour your hands well. Spoon a biscuit-size lump of wet dough into the flour and sprinkle some flour over the wet dough to coat the outside. Pick up the biscuit and shape it roughly into a soft round. At the same time shake off any excess flour. The dough is so soft that it will not hold its shape. As you shape each biscuit, place it in the pan. Push the biscuits tightly against each other so that they will rise up and not spread out. Continue shaping biscuits in this manner until all the dough is used. (To make a large batch of biscuits in a hurry, spray a medium-size—about 2-inch—ice cream scoop with nonstick cooking spray. Cover a jelly roll pan with all-purpose flour. Quickly scoop biscuits onto the flour, sprinkle with flour, shape, and place in small pans.)

✳ Brush the biscuits with melted butter and bake just above the center of the oven until lightly browned, about 15 to 20 minutes. Cool for 1 or 2 minutes in the pan, then dump out and cut the biscuits apart. Split biscuits in half, butter, and eat immediately.

NOTE: If low-protein Southern self-rising flour is not available, use 1 cup all-purpose and 1/2 cup instant (such as Wondra or Shake and Blend) or cake flour, plus 1/2 teaspoon baking powder. If self-rising flour is not available, use a total of 1 1/2 teaspoons baking powder. Do not use self-rising flour for the shaping, since the leavener will give a bitter taste to the outside of the biscuits.

MAKES 10 BISCUITS

THE secret OF THESE FEATHERY BISCUITS IS A dough SO WET THAT IT MUST BE FLOURED IN ORDER TO BE HANDLED. THE LIQUID IN A WET DOUGH SUCH AS THIS TURNS TO steam IN A HOT OVEN, CREATING A POWERFUL LEAVENER.

 **SANDWICHES AND BURGERS**

Stuffed Mediterranean Pita Sandwiches

2 cloves garlic, minced, plus ¼ teaspoon
    oil, or 1 teaspoon prepared minced
    garlic *(see page 13)*
1 tablespoon olive oil
6 large portobello mushrooms, stems
    removed and caps cut into ½-inch-
    thick slices
1½ onions, thinly sliced (approximately
    1½ cups)
1 large head (approximately 1 pound)
    escarole, washed, well dried, and
    coarsely chopped
2 bunches (approximately 1 pound)
    arugula, washed, well dried, and
    coarsely chopped

25 basil leaves (approximately 1 cup)
1 (15-ounce) can chickpeas,
    rinsed and drained
6 ounces feta cheese, preferably
    seasoned with herbs, crumbled
Salt and freshly ground pepper
6 sandwich-size pita rounds, preferably
    whole wheat, cut in half
3 plum tomatoes, cut ¼ inch thick
    (approximately 6 slices each), for
    garnish (optional)

SERVES 6

IF YOU WANT TO serve
THESE SANDWICHES AS
FINGER FOOD, USE
hearty BREAD CUT
INTO SQUARES AND top
WITH THE VEGETABLE
MIXTURE.

✱ In a large nonstick skillet, sauté the garlic in the oil over low heat approximately 1 to 2 minutes, or until aromatic. Add the mushrooms, cover the pan, and cook for approximately 3 minutes, or until soft.

✱ Remove the mushrooms and garlic from the pan and set aside. Add the onions to the pan along with 2 tablespoons of water, cover, and steam for 2 to 3 minutes, or until translucent. Add the greens, basil, and chickpeas to the pan, cover, and continue steaming only until greens wilt, 1 to 2 minutes. Remove from the heat and toss with half of the cheese and the mushrooms. Season with salt and pepper to taste.

✱ To assemble the sandwiches, stuff each pita half with the mushroom and greens mixture and slices of tomatoes, if desired. Garnish with the remaining cheese.

Jerk Chicken Sandwich with
Grilled Pineapple and Colby Cheese

SERVES 6

IF YOU prefer, YOU
CAN SUBSTITUTE CHED-
DAR OR JACK cheese
FOR THE COLBY. YOU
COULD ALSO broil THE
PINEAPPLE INSTEAD OF
GRILLING IT.

Marinade
1 tablespoon olive or vegetable oil
1 cup ketchup
$^1/_2$ teaspoon garlic powder
1 teaspoon dried basil
1 tablespoon jerk seasoning or
   Jamaican spice blend
1 tablespoon lime or lemon juice

6 boneless and skinless chicken breast
   halves (approximately 4 ounces each)
12 slices ($^1/_4$ inch thick) fresh or
   canned pineapple
6 sesame-seeded hoagie rolls (or any
   sandwich bread)
6 ounces Colby cheese, cut into 12 slices
6 large lettuce leaves, for garnish

✳ Mix all the marinade ingredients together in a large bowl. Reserve one-third of the marinade for a sandwich spread. Toss the chicken in the remaining marinade, then place the chicken on a rimmed baking sheet. Set in the refrigerator and marinate for 20 minutes.

✳ While the chicken is marinating, prepare a grill or place a grill pan over high heat.

✳ Brush the pineapple slices with some of the reserved marinade and grill until they turn golden brown and soften slightly, approximately 5 minutes on each side, depending on the thickness.

✳ Preheat the oven to 325°F. Remove the chicken from the marinade, shaking off any excess, place on a baking sheet, and bake for approximately 20 minutes, or until the chicken is done.

✳ Leave the oven on and place the rolls on a sheet pan and toast for 3 to 4 minutes until lightly brown and warmed through. Remove the rolls from the oven and transfer to a cutting board. Brush each roll with some of the reserved marinade. Arrange 1 chicken breast on each roll top, cover with 2 pineapple slices, and then top with 2 slices of cheese. Turn on the broiler, place the sandwiches on the baking sheet, and broil until the cheese melts.

✳ To serve, line the roll bottoms with lettuce and cover with the broiled top halves.

Grilled Beefsteak Sandwich with Wilted Onions and Black Bean Spread

5 large onions, sliced into $1/3$-inch-
 thick rings
1 tablespoon olive oil
2 tablespoons vinegar, preferably cider
1 teaspoon sugar
$1/2$ teaspoon salt
1 teaspoon curry powder (or 1 teaspoon
 cumin plus 1 teaspoon chili powder)
2 tablespoons chopped parsley

Black Bean Spread
1 (19-ounce) can black beans, rinsed and
 drained
1 tablespoon mayonnaise
2 tablespoons vinegar (any kind)
2 to 3 scallions, green parts only
15 to 20 fresh cilantro leaves
$1/2$ teaspoon garlic powder
$1/4$ teaspoon salt

6 (4-ounce) filets of beef tenderloin,
 NY strip, or sirloin steak, all visible
 fat removed
Olive oil
Salt and freshly ground pepper
6 English muffins, split and toasted
12 lettuce leaves, washed and well dried,
 for garnish (optional)
3 large tomatoes, each cut into 8 slices

SERVES 6

THIS sandwich CAN COME TOGETHER QUITE quickly. WHILE THE ONIONS ARE COOKING, GRILL THE STEAK AND prepare THE BLACK BEAN SPREAD.

✴ Place the onions, along with the oil, vinegar, sugar, salt, and curry in a nonstick skillet; stir, cover with a lid and cook over low heat for approximately 6 to 8 minutes, or until cooked but still firm to the bite. Remove from the heat and toss with the parsley. Set aside.

✴ While the onions are cooking, prepare the black bean spread. Place all the spread ingredients in a food processor and blend until smooth and creamy. Set aside. (The spread may be covered and stored in the refrigerator for up to 1 week.)

✴ Prepare a grill or preheat the broiler. Lightly brush the beef with oil, sprinkle with salt and pepper, and grill or broil to the desired doneness, approximately 2 to 3 minutes each side for rare to medium rare. Slice across the grain on a slight diagonal.

✴ To assemble the sandwiches, toast the English muffin halves, then slather some of the Black Bean Spread on both sides. Top each sandwich with some lettuce leaves, tomato slices, sliced beef, and wilted onions.

Lamb Burgers and Potato Petals

Yogurt Sauce
1¹/₂ cups nonfat yogurt or a combination
    of nonfat yogurt and low-fat sour cream
¹/₂ teaspoon salt

Potato Petals
2¹/₂ pounds potatoes (Yukon Golds, Idaho,
    or baking potatoes)
1 tablespoon olive oil
1 teaspoon each: dried thyme, oregano,
    marjoram, salt and pepper, or to taste

Lamb Burgers
4 cloves garlic, peeled
1 medium onion, peeled and roughly
    chopped
1 tablespoon olive oil
1 teaspoon each: ground cumin, ground
    coriander, red pepper flakes, salt and
    pepper, or to taste
1 pound chopped fresh spinach or
    1 (10-ounce) box frozen spinach,
    thawed and squeezed
1 cup unpacked fresh mint leaves, or
    2 tablespoons dried mint
1¹/₂ cups unpacked fresh flat-leaf parsley
    (reserve ¹/₂ cup for garnish)
1¹/₂ pounds ground lamb (if using patties,
    make sure they are not preseasoned)

✳ To make yogurt sauce, mix together yogurt and salt. Set aside in refrigerator.

✳ To make potato petals, slice potatoes on diagonal bias into ¹/₃-inch slices. Lay in a single layer on a baking sheet. Sprinkle and toss with olive oil, herbs, salt and pepper. Set aside.

✳ Start a fire or turn gas grill to medium.

✳ To make burgers, place garlic and onion in a food processor fitted with a metal blade. Pulse until finely chopped.

✳ In a large sauté pan over medium-high heat, warm olive oil. Add garlic and onions, and sauté until translucent, about 3 minutes. Add spices and continue to sauté, stirring often, for another minute (be careful not to burn spices).

✳ Add chopped spinach, mint, and parsley to onion mixture. Stir well, cover, and allow spinach to wilt, about 3 to 5 minutes. Place mixture in a large mixing bowl.

✳ Add ground lamb to onion-spinach mixture and gently mix ingredients together. Form into 6 patties.

✳ Place potatoes on grill and grill for about 7 to 8 minutes per side, until puffed and golden brown. Add patties to grill and cook for about 4 to 5 minutes per side.

✳ To assemble the dish, fan potato slices onto serving plate. Place a burger at the base of each potato fan. Drizzle yogurt sauce over entire plate and garnish with reserved parsley. Serve immediately.

Knecht Burgers

JAMES MCNAIR

1 1/2 pounds ground lean beef
1/4 cup finely chopped yellow onion
2 tablespoons Worcestershire sauce, or
    to taste
Salt

1 sweet French or Italian baguette, about
    2 1/2 inches wide, split lengthwise
Unsalted butter, softened, for spreading
Yellow American or Dijon-style mustard

✳ In a large bowl, combine the beef, onion, Worcestershire sauce, and salt to taste.

✳ Preheat the oven to 400°F. Spread the bread with a thin coating of the butter. Spread the meat mixture over the bread in an even layer about 1/4 inch thick. Be sure that the meat covers the edges of the bread; any exposed bread will burn. Press the meat down around the edges with a fork or your fingers to adhere it to the bread. Spread a thin layer of mustard over the meat. Place the bread on an ungreased baking sheet.

✳ Place the burgers in the hot oven and cook until done to preference, about 6 to 7 minutes for medium-rare.

✳ Transfer the baguette halves to a cutting surface and cut each piece crosswise into 8 equal sections, or as desired.

SERVES 8

THE PROBLEM WITH THESE SAVORY mini-burger APPETIZERS IS THAT THEY DISAPPEAR FASTER THAN YOU CAN MAKE THEM. THE SOLUTION? MAKE scores OF THEM AHEAD OF TIME AND FREEZE.

Three Nut Turkey Burger

JAMES MCNAIR

SERVES 4

THEODORE SKIBA FROM

TEQUESTA, FLORIDA,

WAS awarded THE

JUDGE'S AWARD FOR CRE-

ATIVITY FOR THIS zesty

ENTRY IN THE BUILD-

A-BETTER-burger

CONTEST.

Tropical Fruit Salsa
1 star fruit (carambola)
1 small, ripe mango, peeled, pitted, and
    cut into $1/4$-inch dice
$1/2$ cup red seedless grapes, coarsely
    chopped
1 banana, peeled and cut into $1/2$-inch dice
$1/3$ small cantaloupe, peeled, seeded, and
    cut into $1/4$-inch dice
$1/2$ cup diced ($1/4$-inch) pineapple, fresh or
    canned in its own juices
1 fresh jalapeño pepper, stemmed and cut
    into very small squares

Grated zest and juice of 1 lime
$1/4$ cup freshly squeezed orange juice

Turkey Burgers
$1/2$ cup (about 2 ounces) filberts
$1/2$ cup (about 2 ounces) almonds
$1/2$ cup (about $1 1/2$ ounces) walnuts
1 tablespoon peanut oil
2 cups shredded Monterey Jack cheese
1 pound lean ground turkey
4 whole-wheat hamburger buns, split
Vegetable oil for brushing on grill rack
Red leaf lettuce leaves

✱ To make the salsa, cut half of the star fruit into ¼-inch dice. Slice the remaining star fruit crosswise and reserve for garnish. In a large bowl, combine the remaining salsa ingredients. Stir well to blend, cover, and refrigerate for at least 1 hour or up to 3 hours.

✱ To make the burgers, chop 5 tablespoons of each type of nut. Heat the peanut oil in a medium-size nonstick skillet over medium-high heat. Add the chopped nuts and sauté until lightly toasted, about 5 minutes. Combine the toasted nuts with 1 cup of the cheese and set aside. Grind the remaining nuts together in a food processor and set aside.

✱ Divide the ground turkey into 8 equal portions and form into patties to fit buns. Distribute nut and cheese mixture evenly over the tops of the patties. Cover with the remaining patties and press the edges together to seal. Spread the remaining ground nut mixture on a large, flat plate and press both sides of each burger into the nuts, pressing hard enough for good adhesion.

✱ In a grill with a cover, prepare a hot fire for direct heat cooking.

✱ When the fire is ready, brush the grill rack with vegetable oil. Place the patties on the grill, cover, and cook until browned on the bottom, about 4 minutes. With a wide spatula, turn the patties, replace cover, and cook until juices run clear when the patties are pierced, about 5 minutes longer. During the last few minutes of cooking, distribute the remaining cup of cheese evenly over the tops of the burgers to melt. Place the buns, cut side down, on the outer edge of the grill to lightly toast.

✱ To serve, spoon 2 to 3 tablespoons of the salsa on the bottoms of the buns. Add the patties, top each with about 1 tablespoon of the salsa and a lettuce leaf, and cover with the bun tops. Serve immediately.

New California Patty Melts

JAMES MCNAIR

3 tablespoons unsalted butter
2 cups thinly sliced yellow onion
1 pound ground beef
2 teaspoons Worcestershire sauce, or
    to taste

Salt and freshly ground black pepper
8 rye bread slices
4 ounces creamy goat's milk cheese
Vegetable oil for brushing on grill rack
Variety of mustards for serving

SERVES 4

CHÈVRE AND CARAMEL-
IZED ONIONS ADD
AN updated TASTE
TO THIS LOS ANGELES
classic, USUALLY MADE
WITH CHEDDAR CHEESE
AND grilled ONION.

✳ In a medium-size sauté pan or skillet, melt the butter over medium heat. Add the onion, cover, reduce the heat to low, and cook, stirring from time to time, for 15 minutes. Remove cover, and continue to cook the onion over low heat until very soft and golden, about 45 minutes longer, stirring to keep onions from sticking to pan.

✳ Start a fire in a grill or preheat a broiler.

✳ While onions are cooking and after fire has been lit, combine ground beef, Worcestershire sauce, and salt and pepper to taste in a large bowl. Handling the meat as little as possible to avoid compacting it, mix ingredients together well. Divide the mixture into 8 equal portions and form into thin, round patties to fit the bread slices. Cut the cheese into 4 pieces a little smaller than the patties. Place a piece of cheese on 4 of the patties, cover with the remaining patties, and press edges together to seal and encase the cheese.

✳ When the fire is hot, brush the grill rack or broiler rack with vegetable oil. Place the patties on the grill rack or under the broiler and cook until browned, about 4 minutes. With a wide spatula, turn the patties and cook until done to preference, about 4 minutes longer for medium-rare. During the last few minutes of cooking, place the bread slices on the outer edges of the grill to toast lightly or prepare in toaster.

✳ Top 4 slices of the bread with the patties, pile on the onion, and cover with the remaining bread slices. Offer mustards at the table.

PIZZA

Basic Pizza Dough

JAMES MCNAIR

1 tablespoon sugar
1 cup warm water (110 to 115°F)
1 envelope (¼ ounce) active dry yeast

3¼ cups unbleached all-purpose flour
1 teaspoon salt
¼ cup olive oil, preferably extra-virgin

✳ In a small bowl, dissolve the sugar in the warm water. Sprinkle the yeast over the water and stir gently until it dissolves, approximately 1 minute. Let stand in a warm spot until a thin layer of foam covers the surface, approximately 5 minutes.

✳ **To mix and knead the dough by hand,** combine 3 cups of the flour with the salt in a large mixing bowl. Make a well in the center of the flour and pour in the yeast mixture and the oil. Using a wooden spoon, vigorously stir the flour into the well, beginning in the center and working toward the sides of the bowl, until the flour is incorporated and the soft dough just begins to hold together. Turn the dough out onto a lightly floured surface. Dust your hands with flour and knead the dough gently for 5 minutes, gradually adding just enough of the remaining flour until the dough is no longer sticky. Continue kneading until the dough is smooth, elastic, and shiny, 10 to 15 minutes longer. Knead the dough only until it feels smooth and springy.

✳ **To mix and knead the dough in a food processor,** add 3 cups of the flour and the salt to the work bowl fitted with the metal blade or a dough hook. Pulse for approximately 5 seconds to combine the ingredients. Add the yeast mixture and oil, if desired, and process continuously until the dough forms a single ball, approximately 30 seconds. If the dough is sticky, continue processing while gradually adding just enough of the remaining flour for the dough to lose its stickiness. If the dough is dry and crumbly, gradually add warm water until it is smooth. Turn the dough out onto a lightly floured surface and knead by hand as described above for 2 minutes.

✳ After mixing and kneading the dough, shape the dough, and place it in a well-oiled bowl, turning to coat completely on all sides with oil. Cover the bowl tightly with plastic wrap and set to rise in a warm place until doubled in bulk, approximately 1 to 1½ hours.

✳ Punch down the dough as soon as it has doubled in bulk. Shape it into a ball, pressing out all the air bubbles. To shape a flat pizza, place the ball of dough on a lightly floured surface and dust the top lightly with flour. Using the heels of your hands, press the dough into a circle or other desired shape, then roll it out with a lightly floured rolling pin until it is ¼ inch thick, keeping the edges a little thicker than the center. While rolling, pick up the dough and turn it over several times to stretch it. Rest one hand near the edge of the dough and use the other hand to push the dough against it to form a slight rim around the perimeter of the dough. Fill and bake as quickly as possible.

MAKES 2 (12-INCH) ROUND PIZZAS

THIS versatile DOUGH COMES FROM JAMES MCNAIR'S SEMINAL BOOK ON PIZZA. IT CAN BE USED FOR any TYPE OF PIZZA: TRADITIONAL OR CONTEMPORARY, FLAT OR DEEP-DISH, TOPPED, STUFFED, OR folded. THE RECIPE CAN ALSO BE DOUBLED AND FROZEN FOR future PIZZAS.

Olive Paste Pizza

JAMES MCNAIR

Basic Pizza Dough (see page 79), or approximately 2 pounds purchased dough, or 2 large or 4 to 6 individual-sized prebaked crusts

1 cup pitted imported ripe olives, such as Niçoise

1/2 cup firmly packed fresh basil leaves

3 tablespoons capers, rinsed and drained

2 tablespoons coarsely chopped garlic

1/4 cup olive oil, preferably extra-virgin

Approximately 2 tablespoons freshly squeezed lemon juice

Salt

1/2 teaspoon freshly ground pepper

Vegetable oil for brushing, if using a pizza screen or pizza pan

Cornmeal for dusting, if using a pizza peel

Olive oil, preferably extra-virgin, for brushing crust and drizzling on top

4 cups freshly shredded semisoft cheese such as Morbier, Port-Salut, or Taleggio (approximately 20 ounces)

2 cups (approximately 1 pound) chopped, peeled, and well-drained ripe tomato

1 cup sliced (approximately 1 medium) red onion, separated into half rings

Shredded fresh basil, for garnish

Finely diced fresh red or yellow bell peppers, for garnish

✱ Prepare the Basic Pizza Dough and set it aside to rise. If using purchased dough or prebaked crusts, set aside.

✱ Preheat the oven to 500°F. In a food processor fitted with the metal blade or in a blender, combine the olives, basil leaves, capers, garlic, and the 1/4 cup olive oil. Purée until smooth. Season to taste with lemon juice, salt, and pepper and blend well. Set aside.

✱ Brush a pizza screen or ventilated pizza pan with vegetable oil or dust a pizza peel with cornmeal; set aside. Shape the pizza dough as directed in the basic recipe.

✱ Brush the raw dough or the prebaked crusts all over with olive oil or other vegetable oil, then spread with the olive paste, leaving a 1/2-inch border around the edges. Distribute the cheese over the olive paste, top with the tomato and onion, and drizzle evenly with olive oil.

✱ Transfer the pie to the preheated oven and bake until the crust is crisp and the cheese is bubbly, approximately 8 minutes for prebaked crusts, or 10 to 15 minutes for fresh dough. Remove from the oven to a cutting tray or board and lightly brush the edges of the crust with olive oil. Sprinkle with the shredded basil and diced peppers. Slice and serve immediately.

Banana Satay Pizza

JAMES MCNAIR

Basic Pizza Dough (see page 79), or
approximately 2 pounds purchased
dough

Peanut Sauce
2/3 cup smooth peanut butter
1 1/2 cups homemade or sweetened
canned coconut milk
1/4 cup vegetable stock, preferably
homemade
1/4 cup heavy cream
1/4 cup freshly squeezed lemon juice
2 tablespoons soy sauce
2 tablespoons brown sugar or molasses

1 teaspoon grated fresh ginger
2 teaspoons minced or pressed garlic
Ground cayenne pepper

Vegetable oil for brushing, if using
a pizza screen or pizza pan
Cornmeal for dusting, if using a pizza peel
Canola oil or other high-quality
vegetable oil
6 ripe, yet firm bananas
3 tablespoons unsalted butter, melted,
or more as needed
Chopped roasted peanuts, for garnish
Grated lime zest, for garnish

SERVES 4 TO 6
AS A MAIN COURSE;
8 TO 10 AS AN
APPETIZER

THIS DESSERT pizza,
CREATED BY JAMES
MCNAIR, PAIRS THE
sweet CREAMINESS
OF BANANAS WITH A
spicy SOUTHEAST
ASIAN PEANUT SAUCE.

✷ Prepare the Basic Pizza Dough and set it aside to rise. If using purchased dough, set aside.

✷ Preheat the oven to 500°F. To make the peanut sauce, in a saucepan combine the peanut butter, coconut milk, stock, cream, lemon juice, soy sauce, brown sugar or molasses, ginger, garlic, and cayenne pepper to taste. Place over medium heat and cook, stirring constantly, until the sauce is as thick as a cheese sauce, approximately 15 minutes. Reserve. (This mixture can also be made up to 24 hours ahead, covered, and refrigerated. Return to room temperature before using.)

✷ Brush a pizza screen or ventilated pizza pan with vegetable oil or dust a pizza peel with cornmeal; set aside. Shape the pizza dough as directed in the basic recipe.

✷ Brush the dough all over with the canola oil or other vegetable oil, then top with the peanut sauce, leaving a 1/2-inch border around the edges. Slice the bananas lengthwise or into rounds and distribute them over the sauce. Brush the banana slices with the melted butter.

✷ Transfer the pie to the preheated oven and bake until the crust is crisp, 10 to 15 minutes. Remove from the oven to a cutting tray or board and lightly brush the edges of the crust with canola oil or other vegetable oil. Sprinkle with the peanuts and lime zest. Slice and serve immediately.

Pizza with Garlic-Glazed Chicken

JAMES MCNAIR

SERVES 4 TO 6
AS A MAIN COURSE;
8 TO 10 AS AN
APPETIZER

DON'T BE ALARMED BY
THE huge QUANTITY
OF GARLIC CALLED FOR IN
THIS RECIPE BY JAMES
MCNAIR THE AROMATIC
BULB TURNS SWEET AND
succulent DURING
THE COOKING.

Basic Pizza Dough (see page 79), or
  approximately 2 pounds purchased
  dough
1/4 cup sesame seeds
2 heads garlic, broken into cloves, peeled
  and coarsely chopped
2 teaspoons crushed dried red
  chili pepper
1/2 cup soy sauce
5 tablespoons honey

1 1/2 cups rice vinegar
Approximately 3/4 cup vegetable oil
5 boneless and skinless chicken breast
  halves, cut into bite-sized pieces
Cornmeal for dusting, if using a pizza peel
2 cups (approximately 8 ounces) grated
  Gruyère cheese
1 cup (approximately 4 ounces) shredded
  mozzarella cheese
1/4 cup chopped green onions

✳ Prepare the Basic Pizza Dough and set it aside to rise. If using purchased dough, set aside.

✳ Preheat the oven to 500°F. Place the sesame seeds in a small skillet and toast over medium heat, stirring or shaking the pan, until golden, approximately 4 minutes. Empty onto a plate to cool.

✳ Combine the garlic, crushed red pepper, soy sauce, honey, and vinegar in a bowl.

✳ Heat 1/4 cup of the vegetable oil in a sauté pan or a large skillet over medium-high heat and sauté the chicken until opaque on all sides, approximately 3 minutes. Remove with a slotted spoon and reserve. Pour the garlic mixture into the skillet and cook over medium-high heat, stirring frequently, until the sauce is reduced to the consistency of a syrup, approximately 15 minutes. Return the chicken to the pan and cook, stirring constantly, until the pieces are lightly glazed, approximately 2 minutes. Remove from the heat and reserve.

✳ Brush a pizza screen or ventilated pizza pan with vegetable oil or dust a pizza peel with cornmeal; set aside. Shape the pizza dough as directed in the basic recipe.

✳ Brush the dough all over with vegetable oil, then top with a layer of each of the cheeses and the glazed chicken, leaving a 1/2-inch border around the edges. Sprinkle with the remaining cheese and the green onion and drizzle evenly with olive oil.

✳ Transfer the pie to the preheated oven and bake until the crust is crisp and the cheese is bubbly, approximately 10 to 15 minutes. Remove from the oven to a cutting tray or board and lightly brush the edges of the crust with vegetable oil. Sprinkle with the toasted sesame seeds, slice, and serve immediately.

Salad Pizza

JAMES MCNAIR

Basic Pizza Dough (*see page 79*), or
   approximately 2 pounds
   purchased dough
Vegetable oil for brushing, if using
   a pizza screen or pizza pan
Cornmeal for dusting, if using
   a pizza peel
Olive oil, preferably extra-virgin
1 tablespoon minced or pressed garlic
3 cups freshly shredded mozzarella
   (approximately 12 ounces)
1 cup freshly grated Parmesan cheese,
   preferably Parmigiano-Reggiano
   (approximately 4 ounces)

Balsamic Vinaigrette

2 tablespoons balsamic vinegar
1 teaspoon Dijon-style mustard
$1/2$ teaspoon sugar
$1/4$ teaspoon salt, or to taste
$1/4$ teaspoon freshly ground pepper
$1/4$ cup olive oil, preferably extra-virgin

4 cups small whole or torn tender salad
   greens, rinsed, dried, and chilled
$1/2$ small red onion, cut in half, then thinly
   sliced and separated into half rings
Pesticide-free edible flower petals such as
   nasturtium or calendulas (optional)

✳ Prepare the Basic Pizza Dough and set it aside to rise. If using purchased dough, set aside.

✳ Preheat the oven to 500°F. Brush a pizza screen or ventilated pizza pan with vegetable oil or dust a pizza peel with cornmeal; set aside. Shape the pizza dough as directed in the basic recipe.

✳ Brush each dough round all over with olive oil, then sprinkle with the garlic and top with the mozzarella cheese, leaving a ½-inch border around the edges. Sprinkle with the Parmesan cheese and drizzle evenly with olive oil.

✳ Transfer the pies to the preheated oven and bake until the crusts are crisp and the cheese is bubbly, approximately 10 to 15 minutes.

✳ Meanwhile, to make the vinaigrette, in a bowl or in a jar with a cover combine the vinegar, mustard, sugar, and salt and pepper to taste. Whisk well or cover and shake to blend well. Add the olive oil and whisk or shake until emulsified. Alternatively, the ingredients may be mixed in a food processor or blender.

✳ Just before the pizza is done, combine the salad greens, onion, and flower petals, if desired, in a bowl. Pour on the vinaigrette to taste and toss well.

✳ Remove the pizzas from the oven to a cutting tray or board and lightly brush the edges of the crusts with olive oil. Mound the salad on the pizzas and serve immediately. At the table, slice each pizza in half. Instruct diners to fold each half together around the salad and eat out of hand like a sandwich.

SERVES 4 TO 6
AS A MAIN COURSE;
8 TO 10 AS AN
APPETIZER

THE concept BEHIND THIS JAMES MCNAIR CREATION IS TO TOP A hot CHEESE PIZZA WITH A REFRESHING MOUND OF cool, CRISP SALAD. THE PIE IS THEN folded OVER AND EATEN AS A SANDWICH. FOR VARIETY, SUBSTITUTE YOUR FAVORITE CHEESE AND SALAD DRESSING.

Mozzarella and Tomato Pizza

JAMES MCNAIR

SERVES 4 TO 6
AS A MAIN COURSE;
8 TO 10 AS AN
APPETIZER

THIS RECIPE IS JAMES
MCNAIR'S VERSION OF
THE classic PIZZA
MARGHERITA, ORIGINALLY
CREATED IN honor OF
ITALY'S NINETEENTH-
CENTURY QUEEN
MARGHERITA. IT IS ESSEN-
TIAL THAT YOU USE THE
finest INGREDIENTS—
FRESH CHEESE, VINE-
RIPENED TOMATOES, AND
HIGH-QUALITY OLIVE OIL.

Basic Pizza Dough (see page 79), or approximately 2 pounds purchased dough

Cornmeal, for dusting, if using a pizza peel

Approximately 1/2 cup olive oil, preferably extra-virgin

2 1/2 cups (approximately 10 ounces) shredded fresh mozzarella cheese, preferably imported, made in part from water buffalo's milk

4 cups peeled, seeded, chopped, and well-drained vine-ripened Italian plum tomatoes (approximately 2 pounds), or 1 1/2 (28-ounce) cans Italian plum tomatoes, well drained, seeded, and chopped

1 tablespoon minced fresh oregano, or 1 teaspoon dried oregano

Salt

1/2 cup (approximately 2 ounces) freshly grated Parmesan cheese, preferably Parmigiano-Reggiano

1/2 cup shredded fresh basil (optional)

✱ Prepare the Basic Pizza Dough and set it aside to rise. If using purchased dough, set aside.

✱ Preheat the oven to 500°F. Brush a pizza screen or ventilated pizza pan with vegetable oil or dust a pizza peel with cornmeal; set aside. Shape the pizza dough as directed in the basic recipe.

✱ Brush the dough all over with olive oil, then evenly cover with the mozzarella cheese, leaving a 1/2-inch border around the edges. Cover the cheese with the tomatoes, then sprinkle with the oregano, salt to taste, and about half of the Parmesan cheese. Drizzle evenly with olive oil.

✱ Transfer the pizza to the preheated oven and bake until the crust is golden brown and puffy, approximately 10 minutes. Remove from the oven to a cutting tray or board and lightly brush the edges of the crust with olive oil. Sprinkle with the remaining Parmesan cheese and the shredded basil, if desired. Slice and serve immediately.

Sourdough Pizza with
Potatoes and Caramelized Onions

LORA BRODY

Pizza Dough

1 tablespoon instant active dry yeast

3 cups all-purpose unbleached white flour

1 1/2 teaspoons salt

2 tablespoons Sourdough Bread
  Enhancement Formula™ (see note)

1 cup water, plus 1 to 2 additional
  tablespoons if needed

Toppings

3 Vidalia onions, already caramelized (see
  page 15 for instructions)

1 pound Yukon Gold or Russet potatoes,
  scrubbed

1/4 cup olive oil

Coarse salt and freshly ground pepper

✱ To prepare the dough, place the yeast, flour, salt, Sourdough Bread Enhancement Formula™, and water in a bread machine; program it for Dough or Manual, and press the start button. Add more water if necessary to make a soft, slightly tacky dough. At the end of the final cycle, remove the dough to a lightly floured work surface. The dough will still be quite soft. Knead it by hand for a few minutes, adding only enough flour to make it form a smooth, soft ball. Cover it with a cloth and let it rest on the work surface for 30 minutes. Set aside while you prepare the toppings.

✱ Strain three caramelized onions from the Crock-Pot, cut into thick slices, and set aside.

✱ Place the potatoes in a large pot filled with water and cook for 5 minutes until parboiled. Remove with a slotted spoon and drain well, patting with paper towels. Cut into 1/4-inch-thick slices.

✱ Preheat the oven to 475°F with the rack adjusted in the center position. On a floured surface, stretch or roll out the dough into a 16-inch circle and place it on a perforated or regular pizza pan. Spread with a layer of onions, leaving a 1-inch border around the edge, then top with a layer of potatoes. Drizzle evenly with olive oil and sprinkle with salt and pepper.

✱ Transfer to the preheated oven and bake until the crust is well browned and the potatoes are soft, approximately 20 to 25 minutes. Remove from the oven and place the broiler on high. Broil the pizza for 3 to 4 minutes, or until the potatoes are golden brown and crisp. Serve hot or at room temperature.

NOTE: Sourdough Bread Enhancement Formula™ is available at gourmet food shops nationally.

SERVES 8 TO 10

THIS RECIPE, BY LORA BRODY, DEMONSTRATES THE wonder OF MODERN TECHNOLOGY. YOU'LL NEED A BREAD MACHINE TO MAKE THE PIZZA DOUGH AND A CROCK-POT TO CARAMELIZE THE onions. THE ONIONS MUST BE MADE A DAY IN ADVANCE. THE dough CAN ALSO BE USED TO MAKE BREAD STICKS AS WELL AS ROLLS, LOAVES, AND focaccia. LEAVE THE PEEL ON THE POTATOES—IT IS A GREAT SOURCE OF IRON.

PASTA, NOODLES, AND BEANS

Spaghettini with Red and Gold Cherry Tomatoes

JANET FLETCHER

1/4 pound sweet red cherry tomatoes, halved

1/4 pound small golden cherry tomatoes, halved

3 large shallots, minced

1/4 cup extra-virgin olive oil

Scant 1/4 teaspoon hot red pepper flakes

Salt and freshly ground black pepper

1 pound dried spaghettini or spaghetti

1/2 cup loosely packed fresh basil leaves, stacked a few at a time and cut into thin ribbons

✳ In a large saucepan, combine tomatoes, shallots, olive oil, hot pepper flakes, and salt and pepper to taste. Bring to a simmer over medium heat and simmer until tomatoes render their juices, about 5 minutes. Remove from the heat before the tomatoes completely collapse and lose their shape.

✳ Bring a large pot of salted water to a boil over high heat. Add pasta and cook until al dente. Just before pasta is done, reheat sauce gently. Add basil leaves to sauce. Taste and adjust seasonings.

✳ Drain pasta and return to pot. Add sauce and toss well. Serve on warm plates.

SERVES 4 TO 6

WHEN THE INGREDIENTS ARE FARM-FRESH, EVEN THE simplest OF PASTA DISHES STANDS OUT. THE sauce CAN BE MADE WITH RED TOMATOES ALONE, BUT THE gold TOMATOES ADD EYE APPEAL.

Creamy Pasta Ribbons with Asparagus, Corn, and Sun-Dried Tomatoes

Sauce

4 ounces (1/2 package) Neufchâtel cream cheese, at room temperature

1 (15-ounce) can crushed tomatoes

1 garlic clove, minced, plus 1/8 teaspoon oil, or 1/2 teaspoon prepared minced garlic (see page 13)

1/4 teaspoon salt

1/8 teaspoon coarsely ground fresh pepper

1/2 teaspoon Tabasco sauce

1/2 tablespoon sherry vinegar, or red wine, or tarragon vinegar

1 1/2 pounds wide ribboned pasta noodles

15 sun-dried tomato halves (not packed in oil)

2 cloves garlic, minced, plus 1/4 teaspoon oil, or 1 1/2 teaspoons prepared minced garlic (see page 13)

1 tablespoon olive oil

1/2 small onion, thinly sliced (approximately 1/2 cup)

1 cup reserved pasta water

8 to10 stalks asparagus, ends trimmed off and cut into 2 1/2-inch pieces

1 (11-ounce) can corn

1/4 teaspoon cayenne pepper

1/4 teaspoon salt

1 tablespoon balsamic vinegar

Parmesan cheese curls, for garnish

2 tablespoons sliced scallions, green parts only, for garnish (optional)

* To make the sauce, place the cream cheese, crushed tomatoes, garlic, salt, pepper, Tabasco, and sherry vinegar into a blender and purée until smooth. Set aside.

* Bring a large pot of salted water to a boil and cook the pasta according to the manufacturer's directions until al dente. Reserve the pasta water.

* While the pasta is cooking, rehydrate the sun-dried tomatoes by placing them in a bowl with 1/2 cup water, cover, and microwave for approximately 3 minutes. Alternatively, bring a small pot of water to a boil and add the dry tomatoes. Simmer gently for 1 minute, then remove from the heat and set aside for 5 minutes, or until soft. Drain the rehydrated tomatoes and cut each tomato into 3 strips.

* In a large sauté pan, sauté the garlic in the olive oil over medium heat until golden, approximately 1 to 2 minutes. Add the onion and sauté for 1 minute, or until translucent. Add 3/4 cup of the reserved pasta water to the pan and then add the asparagus. Cover and steam the asparagus until al dente, approximately 3 to 5 minutes.

* Add the rehydrated tomatoes, corn, cayenne, and salt and simmer 1 to 2 minutes until warmed through. Add the drained pasta and vinegar and toss with the sauce, vegetables, and the remaining 1/4 cup reserved pasta water.

* To serve, evenly divide the pasta into 6 serving bowls and garnish each serving with Parmesan curls and scallions.

Bowtie Pasta with Lemon, Capers, Artichokes, and Olives

SERVES 6

THIS quick, COLORFUL, AND EASY PASTA DISH IS A wonderful FIRST COURSE FOR A DINNER PARTY. YOU CAN USE A vegetable STOCK TO MAKE IT AN ALL-VEGETARIAN MEAL. USE half THE AMOUNT OF OLIVES IF YOU ARE CONCERNED ABOUT TOO MUCH SODIUM.

1 1/2 pounds bowtie pasta (also called *farfalle*)

2 cloves garlic, minced, plus 1/4 teaspoon oil, or 1 teaspoon prepared minced garlic *(see page 13)*

1 tablespoon olive oil

2 tablespoons cornstarch

4 tablespoons water

3 cups chicken stock (homemade or low-sodium canned)

1/2 cup green Italian cured olives

1/2 cup black Greek Kalamata or Niçoise olives

1 (14-ounce) can artichoke hearts, rinsed, drained, and quartered (or 6 ounces sugar or snap peas)

1/4 cup capers, finely chopped

Zest and juice of 1 lemon

1/2 cup pimientos, cut into thin strips

1/4 cup chopped scallions, green parts only, for garnish

✳ Bring a pot of water to a boil and cook the pasta according to the manufacturer's directions until al dente.

✳ Meanwhile, in a medium saucepan, sauté the garlic in the olive oil over medium heat until slightly golden, 1 to 2 minutes. In small bowl, mix the cornstarch with the water. Add to the chicken stock, then add the thickened chicken stock to the pan and bring to a boil.

✳ Drain the pasta and place in a large mixing bowl. Add the thickened chicken stock, the olives, artichokes, capers, and lemon zest and juice and toss well.

✳ To serve, evenly divide the pasta into 6 serving bowls and garnish each serving with the pimientos and scallions.

Pasta with Creamy Carrot Sauce and Roasted Peppers

1 pound pasta (any kind)
1 tablespoon olive oil

Creamy Carrot Sauce

1/2 clove garlic, minced, plus 1/4 teaspoon oil, or 1/4 teaspoon prepared minced garlic (see page 13)
1/2 tablespoon orange (or apple) juice concentrate, unreconstituted
2 (4-ounce) jars puréed carrot baby food
1 cup reserved pasta water
1/4 teaspoon salt
1/8 teaspoon dried dill
1/4 cup evaporated skim milk
1 teaspoon rice or apple cider vinegar

2 cloves garlic, minced, plus 1/4 teaspoon oil, or 1 teaspoon prepared minced garlic (see page 13)
1 tablespoon olive oil
5 ounces roasted red peppers or pimientos (packed in water, not marinated)
1 (14-ounce) can artichoke hearts, drained and quartered
1/8 teaspoon freshly ground pepper
1/4 teaspoon dried *fines herbs* mix (optional)
1/2 cup (3 ounces) oil-cured Moroccan olives, pitted
1/4 cup dry-roasted, unsalted peanuts (optional)

✶ Bring a large pot of salted water to a boil and cook the pasta according to the manufacturer's instructions until al dente. Strain and reserve the pasta water. Toss the pasta in the olive oil and set aside.

✶ To make the sauce, in a small saucepan, sauté the 1/2 clove garlic in oil over medium heat until golden, approximately 1 to 2 minutes. Add the orange juice concentrate, puréed carrots, 1/4 cup reserved pasta water, salt, and dill and bring to simmer. Remove the saucepan from the heat and stir in the milk and vinegar. Set aside.

✶ In a separate large sauté pan, sauté the 2 cloves garlic in oil over medium heat until lightly golden brown, approximately 1 to 2 minutes. Add remaining 3/4 cup reserved pasta water, red peppers, artichokes, ground pepper, and *fines herbs* mix, if desired, and simmer gently to heat thoroughly. Remove the pan from the heat and stir in the olives.

✶ In a large pasta bowl, toss the cooked pasta with the sauce and top with the vegetables. Sprinkle with the peanuts, if desired. Serve immediately.

SERVES 4 TO 6

HERE'S A RICH SAUCE MADE without ANY CREAM OR BUTTER. EVERY INGREDIENT CONTRIBUTES TO THE colorful AND DELICIOUS RESULT, INCLUDING THE PURÉED carrots, WHICH ARE ACTUALLY BABY FOOD! IF YOU'RE USED TO CANNED BLACK olives, YOU'LL SEE A BIG DIFFERENCE WITH OIL-CURED Moroccan OLIVES.

Pasta Shells Stuffed with Gorgonzola and Hazelnuts

1 (12-ounce) box jumbo pasta shells

Stuffing
1 tablespoon olive oil
6 cloves garlic, minced
1 (10-ounce) box frozen spinach, defrosted and gently squeezed of excess water
1 pound part-skim ricotta cheese
1/4 pound gorgonzola cheese
1 pound part-skim grated mozzarella
1 teaspoon salt
1/2 teaspoon freshly ground black pepper
1 egg
2 tablespoons milk

4 ounces hazelnuts (walnuts can be substituted)
1 (26-ounce) jar tomato sauce
1 cup grated Parmesan cheese

SERVES 4

HERE'S A great ONE-DISH meal. WALNUTS CAN BE SUBSTITUTED FOR THE HAZELNUTS.

✳ Cook pasta in boiling water according to directions on package. Rinse under cold water and drain well. Set aside.

✳ To make the stuffing, in a medium-size sauté pan, warm oil. Add garlic and cook over a low heat for about 2 minutes. Add spinach and sauté until all excess moisture is cooked out, about 3 to 5 minutes. Place spinach in a large mixing bowl.

✳ Add ricotta, gorgonzola, and half of the mozzarella to spinach in bowl and combine well. Add salt, pepper, egg, and milk and blend all ingredients.

✳ Preheat oven to 350°F. Place nuts on a baking sheet and roast 6 to 8 minutes, shaking pan occasionally, until fragrant. Remove from baking sheet and allow to cool on plate. When cool, roughly chop by hand or in a food processor. Set aside.

✳ Coat a 9 x 13-inch pan with vegetable oil spray. Thinly coat the bottom of the pan with 2 to 3 cups of the tomato sauce, depending upon how saucy you want final dish to be.

✳ With a soup spoon, fill pasta shells with spinach and cheese stuffing. As shells are filled, place in prepared pan, open side up. Top with remaining mozzarella and the Parmesan cheese. Sprinkle with chopped nuts. Bake for 40 to 45 minutes, until bubbly and golden.

Pasta with Tomato Vinaigrette

MICHAEL CHIARELLO

SERVES 6

MICHAEL CHIARELLO, THE CHEF AT TRA VIGNE IN NAPA VALLEY WHO CREATED THIS DISH, insists THAT THE SHAPE OF PASTA YOU USE IS VERY IMPORTANT. SMALL tubes (RIGATONI) AND "LITTLE EARS" (ORECCHIETTE) BOTH HOLD THE SAUCE WELL. IF YOU choose A SMOOTH, STRAIGHT SHAPE SUCH AS SPAGHETTI, THE sauce WILL DRAIN INTO A POOL AT THE BOTTOM OF THE BOWL. THIS PASTA IS MEANT TO BE SERVED JUST SLIGHTLY WARMER THAN ROOM TEMPERATURE.

Basil Oil
2 1/2 cups tightly packed basil leaves
1 1/2 cups olive oil

Tomato Vinaigrette
8 medium vine-ripened red tomatoes, peeled, seeded, and finely chopped
2 tablespoons minced shallots
1 tablespoon minced garlic
6 tablespoons finely chopped fresh flat-leaf parsley

1/4 cup fresh lemon juice
1 cup basil oil (see left) or extra-virgin olive oil
Salt and freshly ground pepper

1 1/2 pounds dried pasta (such as rigatoni or orecchiette)
1 cup freshly grated Parmesan or pecorino cheese

✴ To make your own basil oil, bring a large saucepan of water to a boil. Add the basil and make sure to push the leaves under the boiling water. Blanch the herbs for 5 seconds. Drain into a strainer and immediately plunge into a bowl of ice water. Drain well and squeeze out all the liquid. Purée in a blender with olive oil. Strain the purée immediately through a fine-mesh strainer such as a china cap. Strain again through 4 layers of cheesecloth and put in a sterilized glass bottle. Cover tightly and refrigerate for up to 1 week. *Makes approximately 1 cup oil.*

✴ To make the tomato vinaigrette, in a large nonaluminum bowl, mix together the tomatoes, shallots, garlic, 1/4 cup of the parsley, lemon juice, and basil oil and season with salt and pepper to taste. Set the mixture aside at room temperature for 15 to 20 minutes to let the flavors develop. If making further ahead, do not salt until 15 minutes before serving, otherwise the salt will draw all the water out of the tomatoes.

✴ In the meantime, bring a large pot of salted water to a boil and cook the pasta according to the manufacturer's directions until al dente. Drain well and toss with the tomato vinaigrette. Add 1/2 cup of cheese and mix well.

✴ To serve, evenly divide the pasta into 6 serving bowls and garnish each serving with the remaining cheese and parsley.

Peppered Beef with Flat Rice Noodles

STEVEN WONG

SERVES 4

IN THIS Chinese VERSION OF PEPPER STEAK, THE peppers CAN BE REPLACED WITH CABBAGE OR BROCCOLI.

Marinade

1 tablespoon oyster sauce
1 tablespoon soy sauce
1 teaspoon coarsely ground black pepper
2 tablespoons dry sherry
1 1/2 teaspoons cornstarch

3/4 pound sirloin steak, cut into thin strips

Sauce

1 tablespoon soy sauce
1/4 cup chicken stock

1 pound fresh, flat rice noodles or fresh fettuccine
2 tablespoons vegetable oil
3 tablespoons finely chopped shallots
1 tablespoon finely chopped fresh ginger
1 tablespoon finely chopped garlic
3/4 cup thinly sliced green bell pepper
3/4 cup thinly sliced red pepper
1 cup bean sprouts, packed
Freshly ground black pepper

✶ In a medium bowl, combine all of the marinade ingredients. Add beef strips and marinate for 20 minutes.

✶ In a small bowl, prepare sauce by combining soy sauce and chicken stock. Set aside.

✶ If using fresh rice noodles, break them up by placing in a colander, running hot water over them and separating the strands with your fingers. If using fettuccine, prepare according to package directions, drain, and coat with a little oil.

✶ In a nonstick wok or skillet, heat oil over high heat for 30 seconds. Add shallots, ginger, and garlic and stir-fry for 30 seconds. Add beef and marinade and stir-fry for 2 minutes, stirring to separate pieces. Add peppers and stir-fry 2 minutes longer. Add noodles and sauce, stirring constantly until heated through. Add bean sprouts and mix well. Season to taste with freshly ground pepper and serve immediately.

Satay-Glazed Vegetable Skewers with Cilantro Parmesan Noodles

STEVEN WONG

SERVES 4

SATAY sauce, SOME-
TIMES LABELED CHINESE
BARBECUE SAUCE, IS A
handy PASTRY STAPLE
THAT CAN BE USED TO
GIVE ALMOST ANYTHING A
lift—FROM MEATS AND
SEAFOOD TO VEGETABLES.

1 recipe Cilantro Parmesan Noodles (see page 97)
8 bamboo skewers, soaked in water for 4 hours
2 zucchini, cut into a total of 16 slices, each about 1 inch thick
2 red bell peppers, cut into a total of 16 large squares
16 large mushrooms

Basting Sauce
1 tablespoon satay sauce (Chinese barbecue sauce)
1 tablespoon honey
1 tablespoon hoisin sauce
1 tablespoon soy sauce
1 tablespoon balsamic vinegar

2 tablespoons olive oil

✱ Prepare cilantro parmesan noodles and keep warm.

✱ Preheat broiler or, if using a grill, start fire.

✱ Thread skewers in an attractive arrangement, using 2 pieces of each vegetable for each skewer.

✱ In a small bowl, combine ingredients for basting sauce and mix well.

✱ Brush vegetable skewers with olive oil and broil, or grill for 1 minute on each side. Baste each side with sauce and continue cooking for another 2 minutes on each side or until vegetables are just tender. Continue to baste during cooking to ensure that the vegetables are well coated.

✱ Divide cilantro parmesan noodles among 4 plates. Top with cooked vegetables and serve immediately.

Cilantro Parmesan Noodles

STEVEN WONG

1 pound fresh Shanghai noodles or
  fresh fettuccine

2 tablespoons heavy cream

$^1/_2$ cup freshly grated Parmesan cheese

$^1/_2$ cup chopped cilantro

Salt and freshly ground black pepper

✱ In a large pot of boiling salted water, cook noodles until al dente, about 3 minutes (if cooking fettuccine, prepare according to package directions). Drain.

✱ Immediately return noodles to pot. Over low heat, add cream and Parmesan and mix. Add cilantro and toss thoroughly to combine. Season with salt and pepper to taste. Serve immediately.

SERVES 4

THIS QUICK AND easy NOODLE DISH IS A GOOD ONE TO HAVE IN YOUR repertoire. SERVE WITH GRILLED CHICKEN AND A GREEN SALAD, OR WITH SATAY-GLAZED VEGETABLE skewers.

Four-Bean Meatless Chili

1 cup partially cooked dry bulgur
3 cups boiling water

Chili
2 tablespoons olive oil
4 garlic cloves, minced, plus 1/2 teaspoon oil, or 2 teaspoons prepared minced garlic (see page 13)
3 onions, cut into 1/2-inch dice
10 ounces (3 cups) mushrooms of your choice, cut into 1/2-inch dice
2 teaspoons chili powder
1 teaspoon ground ancho chili or chopped jalapeño

1 teaspoon ground cumin
1/2 teaspoon red pepper flakes
1 teaspoon paprika
2 (16-ounce) cans chopped tomatoes
4 (15-ounce) cans of different beans (such as white and red kidney, pinto, and black), rinsed and drained
1 3/4 cups chicken stock (homemade or low-sodium canned)
1 tablespoon cider or red wine vinegar
1 teaspoon salt
1/4 cup fresh cilantro leaves, for garnish (optional)

✱ Rinse the bulgur under cold running water to remove any dust. Drain, then put the bulgur in a bowl, add the boiling water, and let soak for 30 minutes. If necessary, drain the bulgur and squeeze to remove excess moisture. Fluff the grains with a fork. Set aside.

✱ While the bulgur is soaking, make the chili: In a Dutch oven, heat the olive oil and sauté the garlic and onions together over medium heat until translucent, approximately 3 to 5 minutes. Add the mushrooms and spices and cook for 5 minutes, or until browned. Add the tomatoes, beans, and stock, cover, and simmer for 15 minutes to warm all the ingredients through. Do not excessively stir the mixture or you will mash the beans. Stir in the vinegar and salt.

✱ To serve, spoon the chili into large soup plates. Mound 1/2 cup of cooked bulgur in the center of each and garnish with whole cilantro leaves, if desired.

SERVES 6

WITH THE versatile TASTE THAT COMES FROM USING FOUR DIFFERENT KINDS OF beans, YOU WON'T MISS THE MEAT IN THIS CHILI. IF YOU HAVEN'T EXPERIMENTED WITH BULGUR, YOU'LL FIND IT AN incredibly EASY-TO-MAKE GRAIN THAT GOES WONDERFULLY well WITH CHILI.

Tuscan Salad of Chicory, White Beans, and Hearts of Palm

CLAIRE CRISCUOLO

SERVES 8

THE gourmet OR IMPORT SECTIONS OF MOST SUPERMARKETS CARRY hearts OF PALM PACKED IN CANS OR JARS.

1 medium head of chicory, cut into bite-size pieces

1 head of endive, cut into bite-size pieces

1 small head radicchio, cut into bite-size pieces

4 radishes, thinly sliced

1/2 small cucumber, peeled, seeded, and diced

7 ounces canned hearts of palm, drained and cut into 1/4-inch slices

1 cup freshly cooked or canned white beans, drained (*see cooking directions for dried beans below*)

1/2 small, sweet onion, sliced thinly

2 large cloves garlic, minced

3 tablespoons extra-virgin olive oil

1 lemon, squeezed (about 4 tablespoons juice)

Salt and freshly ground black pepper

✳ Place the chicory, endive, radicchio, radishes, cucumber, hearts of palm, beans, onion, and garlic in a large salad bowl. Toss well using two spoons. Drizzle the olive oil evenly over the salad. Toss to coat the leaves evenly. Drizzle the lemon juice over the salad. Toss well to mix evenly. Add salt and pepper to taste. Toss again to mix well.

NOTE: To cook dried beans, carefully pick through beans to remove any foreign bits or imperfect beans. Place in a large bowl and cover with water by 3 inches. Let stand for several hours or, preferably, overnight.

Drain beans, rinse, and drain again. Transfer beans to a large heavy-bottomed pot. Add enough water to cover by about 1 inch and stir well. Bring to a boil. Using a wire skimmer or slotted utensil, remove any foam that rises to the surface.

Boil for 10 minutes, reduce heat to a gentle simmer, and cover partially. Simmer for 45 minutes to 1½ hours, until beans are tender but still hold their shape.

POULTRY AND SEAFOOD

Braised Farmhouse Chicken

TOM LACALAMITA

2 chicken breasts with bone, split (about
   2 pounds)
1/2 cup water
1/2 cup dry white wine
1/2 cup olive oil
1 bay leaf

8 cloves garlic, unpeeled
1 teaspoon paprika
2 teaspoons salt
1 tablespoon whole black peppercorns
4 threads saffron (optional)

✹ Remove and discard all the visible fat from the chicken. Cut the breast halves into 2 or 3 pieces, right through the bone. Place chicken in a pressure cooker. Add the remaining ingredients and stir to blend.

✹ Position the lid and lock in place. Place over high heat and bring to high pressure. Adjust the heat to stabilize the pressure and cook 15 minutes. Remove from heat and lower pressure using cold-water release method (see note on page 143). Open the pressure cooker.

✹ Place the pressure cooker, uncovered, on a burner over high heat and reduce the sauce by half. Stir periodically so that the chicken does not stick. Taste and adjust for salt.

✹ If serving with fried potatoes, place the potatoes on a large serving platter. Lay the chicken pieces on top of potatoes. Strain sauce to remove peppercorns and bay leaf and spoon the sauce over chicken and potatoes.

SERVES 4

AS THE CHICKEN BRAISES IN THE PRESSURE COOKER, THE cooking LIQUID COMBINES WITH THE NATURAL juices OF THE CHICKEN TO PRODUCE A FLAVORFUL, RICH SAUCE, WHICH IS TRADITIONALLY SERVED OVER MATCHSTICK-THIN potatoes FRIED WITH WHOLE, UNPEELED CLOVES OF GARLIC.

Chicken with Yogurt and Beer

TOM LACALAMITA

2 chicken breasts, split (about 2 pounds)
3 tablespoons olive oil
1 large onion, cut in half and thinly sliced
1 cup plain yogurt
$1/2$ cup beer

$1/2$ teaspoon paprika
$1/2$ teaspoon oregano
$1 1/2$ teaspoons salt
$1/8$ teaspoon freshly ground black pepper

✳ Remove and discard the skin and any visible fat from the chicken. Cut the breast halves into 3 or 4 small pieces, cutting straight through the bone.

✳ Heat the olive oil in a pressure cooker over high heat. Add the chicken a few pieces at a time and brown evenly on all sides. Remove and set aside on a large plate or platter. Reduce heat to medium, add onion, and sauté for 4 to 5 minutes, or until soft. Stir frequently so that the onion does not brown.

✳ Add chicken back to pressure cooker along with any collected juices. Add remaining ingredients and stir well.

✳ Position the pressure cooker lid and lock in place. Raise the heat to high and bring to high pressure. Adjust the heat to stabilize the pressure and cook for 15 minutes. Remove from heat and lower pressure using the cold-water release method (see note on page 143). Open the pressure cooker.

✳ Place the pressure cooker, uncovered, on a burner over high heat and reduce the sauce by half. Stir periodically so the chicken does not stick. Serve immediately.

Pacific Coast Chicken with Jicama-Cucumber Slaw

Marinade

2 teaspoons ground cumin

4 cloves garlic, minced, plus 1/2 teaspoon oil, or 2 teaspoons prepared minced garlic (see page 13)

1/4 teaspoon red pepper flakes

1/2 teaspoon dried thyme

1/2 teaspoon dried sage

1/2 cup pineapple juice

1/2 cup apricot nectar

1/2 cup (1 lime) lime juice

2 tablespoons olive or vegetable oil

1/2 teaspoon freshly ground pepper

1 teaspoon salt

6 (4-ounce) boneless and skinless chicken breast halves

Slaw

1/2 jicama (approximately 7 ounces) or white turnip, peeled, and cut into matchsticks

1 large cucumber, peeled, seeded, and thinly sliced on the diagonal

6 to 8 radishes, halved and thinly sliced

2 tablespoons chopped scallions, green parts only, for garnish

Freshly cracked pepper

✱ Preheat the oven to 325°F. Place the cumin, garlic, red pepper flakes, thyme, and sage in an ovenproof sauté pan, and toast in the oven for 5 to 6 minutes, or until aromatic.

✱ Mix all the marinade ingredients together and divide into 2 separate bowls. Add the chicken to one bowl, turn to coat well, and set in the refrigerator to marinate for at least 20 minutes or overnight. Place the slaw vegetables in the bowl with the other half of the marinade, toss well, and set in the refrigerator for up to 2 hours.

✱ Prepare a grill or preheat the broiler. Shake the excess marinade off the chicken and grill or broil until golden, approximately 3 to 5 minutes each side, or until cooked through.

✱ To serve, mound 1/4 cup of the slaw in the center of each plate. Slice each chicken breast on the bias into 3 or 4 medallions and arrange them next to the slaw. Garnish with the scallions and freshly cracked pepper.

SERVES 6

IN THIS RECIPE, THE MARINADE ACTS AS A flavor enhancer FOR THE CHICKEN AND A dressing FOR THE SLAW. FOR FOOD SAFETY, IT'S IMPORTANT TO divide THE MARINADE INTO TWO BOWLS—ONE FOR THE CHICKEN AND ONE FOR THE SLAW—SO THAT THE CHICKEN MARINADE IS NOT reused. YOU CAN MARINATE THE CHICKEN overnight FOR EVEN MORE FLAVOR.

Crusty Coconut Chicken with
Grilled Pineapple and Chayote

Marinade
3 tablespoons Dijon-style mustard
3 tablespoons apricot preserves
1 tablespoon sesame oil
$1/4$ teaspoon red pepper flakes
$1/4$ teaspoon salt

6 (4-ounce) boneless and skinless chicken breast halves

Crust
$1/2$ cup sweetened shredded coconut
1 cup crushed cornflakes

1 whole fresh pineapple, peeled and cut into $3/4$-inch-thick slices
2 chayotes, peeled, pitted, and sliced into $3/4$-inch-thick wedges

✴ In a large bowl, combine all the marinade ingredients, place the chicken in the bowl, and coat well. Place the bowl in the refrigerator and allow the chicken to marinate for 20 minutes.

✴ In a shallow bowl, mix the coconut and cornflakes together. Remove the chicken from the marinade, shaking off any excess, and roll the chicken into the cornflake mix, coating evenly on all sides. Reserve the marinade.

✴ Preheat the oven to 325°F. Place the chicken on a baking sheet and bake for 20 minutes, or until cooked through. Raise the heat to 400°F and cook for an additional 5 minutes to crisp the crust.

✴ Prepare a grill. In a sauce pot, bring the reserved marinade to a boil and cook for 2 minutes. Brush the fresh pineapple and chayote slices with the cooked marinade. Place directly on the grill and cook until golden in color and softened slightly but not mushy, approximately 3 to 5 minutes on each side.

✴ To serve, slice each chicken breast in half on the bias and arrange the two halves, alternately with slices of grilled pineapple and chayote, on each plate.

Southwestern Chipotle Chicken

SERVES 6

SERVE THIS FLAVORFUL stewed DISH OVER WHITE RICE.

Braising Liquid

1/2 cup tequila, vodka, or white wine

2 tablespoons olive oil

1/2 cup fresh cilantro leaves

1 whole canned chipotle chili in adobo
with 2 teaspoons of the sauce, or
1 fresh jalepeño chili plus 1 drop of
Liquid Smoke™

3 cloves garlic

2 large whole plum tomatoes

4 tablespoons red wine or cider vinegar

4 tablespoons dark Karo syrup, honey, or
maple syrup

4 tablespoons apple juice concentrate

1 teaspoon salt

Zest of 1 lime (or lemon)

Flour, for dredging

1 1/2 pounds boneless and skinless chicken
breast or chicken parts cut into strips

1 tablespoon olive or vegetable oil

1 red onion, cut into large dice

3 large red potatoes, cut into large dice

1/2 pound parsnips, peeled and cut into
1-inch chunks

Juice of 1 lime (or lemon)

Fresh cilantro leaves, for garnish
(optional)

✹ Place all the braising liquid ingredients in a food processor fitted with a metal blade and pulse until smooth. Set aside.

✹ Place the flour in a large shallow bowl. Dredge the chicken strips in the flour, shaking off any excess flour. In a large, ovenproof, nonstick skillet over medium-high heat, sauté the chicken in the oil for 2 to 3 minutes on each side, or until dark golden brown. Remove from the pan and set aside.

✹ Add the onion to pan, lower to medium heat, and sauté approximately 5 minutes until slightly caramelized, stirring constantly to prevent the onion from sticking to the bottom of the pan.

✹ Preheat the oven to 325°F.

✹ Add the potatoes, parsnips, and the braising liquid to the pan and bring to a boil. Place the chicken on top of the vegetables and cover the pan with a tightly fitting lid. Place the pan in the oven and braise for 35 to 40 minutes, or until the vegetables are tender and the chicken is cooked through. After 20 minutes of braising, stir the contents from top to bottom, to ensure even cooking.

✹ To serve, spoon the vegetables from the pan and evenly distribute onto 6 plates. Top with the chicken and some sauce and drizzle some lime juice on top. Garnish with cilantro leaves, if desired.

Chinese-Style Asparagus Chicken

Flour, for dredging
6 (4-ounce) boneless and skinless chicken
 breast halves
2 tablespoons vegetable oil
1/2 cup sliced almonds
3 cloves garlic, minced, plus 1/3 teaspoon
 oil, or 1 1/2 teaspoons prepared minced
 garlic (see page 13)
1/2 tablespoon chopped ginger or
 1/2 teaspoon powdered ginger

4 tablespoons green onions, green parts
 only, chopped
1 1/2 pounds asparagus, trimmed and
 cut into 2-inch pieces
1/2 cup chicken stock (homemade or
 low-sodium canned)
2 tablespoons soy sauce
1/2 teaspoon red pepper flakes or hot bean
 paste (available in Asian markets)
1 tablespoon vinegar, preferably rice wine

✱ Preheat the oven to 350°F. Place the flour in a shallow bowl, dredge the chicken in flour, coating both sides, and shake off any excess. In a large sauté pan over medium-high heat, sauté the chicken in the oil until golden, approximately 3 to 4 minutes on each side. Transfer the chicken from pan to a baking sheet and finish cooking in the oven for approximately 10 minutes, or until cooked through. Set aside.

✱ While the oven is still on, place the almonds on a baking sheet and toast for approximately 10 minutes, or until golden and aromatic. Set aside.

✱ Add the garlic, ginger, and 3 tablespoons of the green onions to the original sauté pan and cook over medium heat for 1 minute, or until they release their aroma. Add the asparagus and 1/4 cup of stock, cover, and steam for 2 minutes, or until done but still firm.

✱ Stir in the soy sauce, pepper flakes, vinegar, and remaining stock, bring to boil, and remove the pan from the heat.

✱ To serve, slice each chicken breast on the bias into 3 or 4 medallions and fan them across each plate. Drizzle the sauce on top and garnish with the reserved green onions and toasted almonds.

Grilled West Indies Spice-Rubbed Chicken Breast with Grilled Banana

CHRIS SCHLESINGER AND JOHN WILLOUGHBY

SERVES 4

THE NORMAL searing AND CRUSTING ACTION OF GRILLING IS ENHANCED BY THE spice RUB, AND THE RESULT IS A SUPERCRUSTED, FLAVOR-CONCENTRATED SURFACE covering A MOIST BREAST.

Spice Rub
3 tablespoons curry powder
3 tablespoons ground cumin
2 tablespoons allspice
3 tablespoons paprika
2 tablespoons powdered ginger
1 tablespoon cayenne pepper
2 tablespoons salt
2 tablespoons freshly ground black pepper

4 boneless chicken breasts, skin on
4 firm bananas, skin on and halved
    lengthwise
2 tablespoons vegetable oil
1 tablespoon soft butter
2 tablespoons molasses

Lime halves for garnish

✻ Mix all the spices together well, rub this mixture over both sides of each chicken breast, cover, and refrigerate for 2 hours.

✻ Start a fire or turn a gas grill to medium.

✻ Over a medium fire, grill the chicken breasts, skin side down, for 7 to 8 minutes, until well browned and heavily crusted. Turn them and grill an additional 10 minutes. Check for doneness by nicking the largest breast at the fattest point: the meat should be fully opaque with no traces of red. Remove chicken from the grill.

✻ Rub the banana halves with the vegetable oil and place them on the grill, flat side down. Grill them for about 2 minutes, or until the flat sides are slightly golden in color. Flip them and grill for an additional 2 minutes.

✻ Remove the banana halves from the grill. Mix the butter and molasses together and paint this over the bananas. Serve the chicken breasts and banana halves together, sprinkled with a little lime juice.

Narsai's Assyrian Chicken

NARSAI DAVID

2 whole boneless, skinless chicken breasts,
   split into halves
3 tablespoons vegetable oil
Salt
Flour
1 cup orange juice

$1/2$ cup white wine
Juice of one lemon
3 tablespoons honey
$1/2$ teaspoon ground ginger
Tabasco sauce or cayenne pepper, to taste
12 kumquats, thinly sliced

✳ Carefully pull away the "fillet" from each half breast (this is a small, elongated section attached to each breast half, sometimes referred to as a "supreme"). Cut the remaining breast meat into 3 or 4 strips the same size as the fillet.

✳ Heat the oil in a large skillet. While it is heating, salt the chicken pieces and flour them very lightly, shaking off any excess flour. (A good way to do this is to put the flour in a paper bag, add several pieces of chicken at a time, close the top, and shake well.) Sauté the chicken in the hot oil only until the pieces are heated through and have turned opaque. It is important to avoid overcooking them. Transfer the chicken pieces to a warm platter.

✳ Add the orange juice, wine, lemon juice, honey, ginger, and Tabasco sauce (or cayenne pepper) to the pan. Whisk to dissolve all the pan drippings and cook, uncovered, until liquid reduces to a thin sauce, about 5 minutes over high heat. Add the kumquats and return the chicken pieces to the pan. Stir just long enough to coat the chicken pieces with the sauce. Serve immediately.

SERVES 6

NARSAI DAVID, OF ASSYRIAN DESCENT, USED HIS **mother's** COOKING AS AN **inspiration** FOR THIS FRUITY AND COLORFUL DISH.

Tuscan Chicken with Creamy White Wine Sauce

6 (4-ounce) boneless and skinless chicken breast halves
Salt and freshly ground pepper
Flour, for dredging
2 tablespoons plus 2 teaspoons olive oil
6 cloves garlic, minced, plus ³/₄ teaspoon oil, or 3 teaspoons prepared minced garlic (see page 13)
1 onion, cut into small dice
1 teaspoon dried thyme

¹/₂ cup white wine
12 sun-dried tomatoes (not packed in oil)
1 cup heavy cream
2 tablespoons chopped fresh parsley
3 ounces cooked ham, such as Canadian bacon or Boar's Head, cut into thin strips
1 (15-ounce) can artichoke hearts, rinsed, drained, and quartered

✻ Season the chicken with salt and pepper. Place the flour in a shallow bowl, dredge the chicken in the flour, and shake off any excess.

✻ Preheat the oven to 325°F. In a large sauté pan, sauté chicken in 2 tablespoons of the olive oil over medium-high heat until brown, approximately 3 to 4 minutes. Transfer the chicken from the pan to a baking sheet and finish cooking in the oven for approximately 10 minutes, or until cooked through. Set aside.

✻ Add the garlic to the original sauté pan and sauté in the remaining 2 teaspoons of oil over low heat for 1 to 2 minutes, or until it becomes aromatic. Add the onion and continue to sauté for 3 to 4 minutes, or until brown. Add the thyme and sauté for an additional 1 minute until it releases its aroma.

✻ Pour in the white wine and deglaze the pan by using a wooden spoon and scraping the bits that have stuck to the pan. Cook over medium heat until the liquid is reduced in volume by half, approximately 2 to 3 minutes.

✻ To rehydrate the sun-dried tomatoes, bring a small pot of water to a boil and add the dry tomatoes. Simmer gently for 1 minute, then remove from the heat and set aside for 5 minutes, or until soft. Drain the rehydrated tomatoes and slice into strips.

✻ Add the cream to the sauce and season with salt and pepper to taste. Gently simmer over low heat for approximately 5 minutes or until the sauce thickens slightly and coats the back of a spoon. Add the tomatoes, parsley, ham, and artichokes to the pan and simmer for 1 to 2 minutes just to warm through.

✻ To serve, slice each chicken breast on the bias into 3 or 4 medallions and fan them across each plate. Arrange the vegetables around the chicken and drizzle the sauce over the vegetables.

Monterey Stuffed Chicken Breasts

DENIS BLAIS

Filling

4 ounces leaf spinach
4 tablespoons butter
2 shallots, minced
1/4 pound sliced mushrooms
1/4 cup julienned sun-dried tomatoes
1 pound ricotta cheese
1/3 cup Parmesan cheese
1 teaspoon finely chopped dill
1 teaspoon finely chopped oregano
1 clove garlic, minced
Salt and freshly ground black pepper
   to taste
2 tablespoons bread crumbs

6 boneless chicken breasts (inside fillet
   attached)
Salt and freshly ground black pepper

White Wine Dill Sauce

4 tablespoons butter
2 large shallots, minced
1 clove garlic, minced
1/4 cup white wine
1 1/2 cups brown veal stock
Juice of 1/2 lemon
1/3 cup heavy cream
1 tablespoon chopped fresh dill

* To prepare filling, blanch spinach in boiling, salted water for 10 to 15 seconds. Drain and cool under cold water. Squeeze out all excess moisture and chop coarsely.

* Warm butter in a small sauté pan. Add shallots and mushrooms and sauté over medium-high heat for 4 to 5 minutes, until soft. Drain in a sieve, reserving a couple tablespoons of the butter and set aside.

* Combine spinach, shallots, mushrooms, and the rest of the filling ingredients in a large mixing bowl. Mix thoroughly.

* Preheat oven to 350°F. Holding each chicken breast pointed end down, firmly open cavity behind the inside fillet. Pack filling deep into cavity until plump. Use skin and fillet to tuck filling in.

* Place stuffed chicken breasts on a baking sheet. Brush with reserved butter and season with salt and pepper. Bake for 30 to 35 minutes, while making white wine dill sauce.

* To make white wine dill sauce, warm butter in a medium sauté pan. Add shallots and garlic and sauté over medium-high heat for 3 to 4 minutes, until soft. Add wine to deglaze pan, stirring with a wooden spoon to pick up any browned bits on the bottom of the pan. Add veal stock, bring to a boil, lower to a simmer, and reduce liquid by half.

* Add lemon juice and cream, bring to a simmer, and simmer to reduce until sauce is thick and shiny.

* Strain sauce through a fine-mesh sieve. Add dill and season with salt and pepper. Serve immediately over chicken breasts.

SERVES 6

DENIS BLAIS, ONE OF VANCOUVER'S finest CHEFS, RECOMMENDS THIS RECIPE FOR home cooks WHO WANT TO MAKE SOMETHING ELEGANT AND EASY.

Rice-Encrusted Chicken with Pears and Blue Cheese

Crust

Flour, for dredging

1 egg plus 2 egg whites, beaten

1 1/2 cups cooked storebought wild rice mix (see sidebar)

6 (4-ounce) boneless and skinless chicken breast halves

Salt and freshly ground pepper

3 tablespoons oil

2 garlic cloves, minced, plus 1/4 teaspoon oil, or 1 teaspoon prepared minced garlic (see page 13)

1 onion, finely chopped (approximately 1 cup)

1 cup white wine (or 1/2 cup apple jack brandy and 1/2 cup chicken stock)

3 ripe but firm Bosc pears, peeled, quartered, and sliced

1/2 red bell pepper, thinly sliced

1/2 cup crumbled blue cheese, such as Maytag

3 tablespoons chopped fresh parsley

Salt and freshly ground pepper

SERVES 6

THIS IS A **perfect** DISH TO MAKE WHEN YOU HAVE **leftover** WILD RICE. OTHERWISE, PREPARE A BOX OF **wild** RICE MIX ACCORDING TO THE MANUFACTURER'S IN- STRUCTIONS, OMITTING THE SEASONING PACKET.

✱ Set up three shallow bowls. Place the flour in one, the beaten egg in the second, and the rice mix in the third. Season the chicken with salt and pepper, dredge the chicken in the flour and shake off any excess; then dip the chicken in the beaten egg and roll in the rice mix to coat evenly.

✱ Preheat the oven to 325°F. In a large sauté pan, cook the chicken in the oil over medium-high heat until brown on all sides, approximately 4 to 5 minutes. Transfer the chicken from the pan to a baking sheet and finish cooking in the oven for approximately 10 minutes, or until cooked through. Set aside.

✱ Add the garlic to the sauté pan and sauté over low heat for 1 to 2 minutes, or until aromatic. Add the onion and continue sautéing over medium heat until it turns brown, approximately 5 minutes.

✱ Add the wine and deglaze the pan by using a wooden spoon and scraping up the bits that have stuck to the pan. Add the pears and red pepper, and bring to a boil. Cover, and cook over medium heat until the liquid is reduced in volume by half and the pears are tender, approximately 5 to 10 minutes. (If the pears are somewhat hard and underripe, add up to another 1/4 cup of wine and cook them for a longer period.)

✱ Remove the pan from the heat, add the blue cheese, and stir until the cheese begins to melt. (You want to have some chunks.) Add 2 tablespoons of parsley, and season with salt and pepper.

✱ To serve, divide the pear mixture evenly and place in the center of each plate. Drizzle some sauce around the pears. Slice each chicken breast on the bias into 3 or 4 medallions and arrange them on top of the pears. Garnish with the remaining parsley.

Dried Apricot, Ham, and
Leek-Stuffed Chicken Breasts

MARLENE SOROSKY

SERVES 8

THIS IS A no-fail,
SUREFIRE, PREPARE-AHEAD
CHICKEN DISH FROM
ENTERTAINING maven
MARLENE SOROSKY. THE
CHICKEN BREASTS ARE
filled WITH A SMOKY-
FRUITY STUFFING,
WRAPPED IN A DELICATE
CRUST, AND TOPPED
WITH AN orange-
tinged SAUCE.

8 (6-ounce) large boneless, skinless
    chicken breast halves

Marinade
1 1/2 cups orange juice
1 cup chicken stock (homemade or low-
    sodium canned)
1/2 cup imported dry vermouth or dry
    white wine
1/4 cup soy sauce
2 tablespoons Dijon mustard
1 tablespoon honey

Stuffing
1/3 cup dried apricots (approximately 10)
2 tablespoons golden raisins

3 medium leeks, cleaned and thickly sliced
4 ounces lean smoked ham or Canadian
    bacon, cut into 1-inch pieces
    (approximately 1 cup)
2 tablespoons olive oil
1/3 cup dry bread crumbs, toasted

Crust
3/4 cup chopped shelled pistachios,
    hazelnuts, or almonds, toasted
1 1/4 cups dry bread crumbs, toasted
Salt and freshly ground pepper

Sauce
1/4 cup heavy cream
4 teaspoons cornstarch

✴ Cut off all fat from chicken. Cut a pocket horizontally into each breast by holding the knife parallel to the counter and cutting back as far as possible without cutting it in half. Leave a small edge uncut on 3 sides. Place in a shallow glass casserole or large plastic zipper bag.

✴ Whisk all the marinade ingredients in a medium bowl. Pour 1 1/4 cups over the chicken, turning to coat all surfaces. Refrigerate for 4 to 12 hours, turning occasionally. Refrigerate the remaining marinade.

✴ To make the stuffing, in a food processor with the metal blade, pulse the apricots until coarsely chopped. Add the raisins, leeks, and ham and pulse until diced into 1/4-inch pieces. In a large skillet, preferably nonstick, heat the olive oil over moderate heat. Add the apricot mixture and bread crumbs and sauté until the leeks are soft and the mixture is lightly browned, 5 to 7 minutes. Stir in 2 tablespoons of the reserved marinade. Cool. (The stuffing may be refrigerated overnight.)

✴ Remove the chicken from the marinade; do not dry. Discard the marinade. Fill each pocket with approximately 2 tablespoons of stuffing. Press the edges to close.

✴ To make the crust, in a pie plate or other shallow dish, stir together the nuts and bread crumbs. Sprinkle the chicken with salt and pepper. Dip both sides into the crumbs, pressing to adhere. Place the chicken breasts at least 1 inch apart on a greased or foil-lined and greased baking sheet. Refrigerate until ready to bake. (The chicken may be refrigerated overnight.)

✴ To make the sauce, pour the reserved marinade into a small saucepan. Simmer for 2 to 3 minutes. Remove from the heat. In a small bowl, stir the cream and cornstarch together; then whisk into the sauce. Return the pan to the heat and bring to a boil, whisking constantly. (The sauce may be refrigerated overnight.)

✴ Place the oven rack in the upper third of the oven and preheat to 450°F. Sprinkle the tops of the chicken breasts with the remaining crumbs and spray with no-stick cooking spray. Bake the chicken for 12 to 15 minutes, or until cooked through.

✴ To serve, arrange the chicken breasts on each plate and drizzle with some sauce. Pass the remaining sauce at the table.

Jerk Chicken

LORA BRODY

SERVES 4

THINK OF COMING HOME FROM A long DAY AT WORK TO A CROCK-POT FULL OF A great CHICKEN DISH. YOU CAN ADJUST THE HEAT OF THIS dish BY ADDING FEWER CHILIES. RICE ACTS AS A nice ACCOMPANIMENT TO THE CHICKEN AND ITS SAUCE.

1 chicken (about 3 1/2 pounds), skin removed and cut into 8 pieces
1 large onion, cut into 8 pieces
3 cloves garlic, peeled
1 generous tablespoon candied ginger
1 1/2 tablespoons canned chipotle chilies, or more to taste

1/2 teaspoon allspice
2 tablespoons mustard
1 teaspoon pepper
2 tablespoons balsamic vinegar
2 tablespoons soy sauce

✳ Place chicken in Crock-Pot.

✳ To prepare the sauce, place onion, garlic, and ginger in a food processor fitted with a metal blade. Process to pulverize. Add the rest of the ingredients to the food processor and pulse to combine.

✳ Pour sauce over chicken in Crock-Pot and toss to coat.

✳ Cook chicken on a low setting for 6 to 8 hours, or on high for 2 to 3 hours.

Chicken Cutlets with Prosciutto and Sage

JAMES MCNAIR

4 boneless, skinless chicken breast halves
Salt
Freshly ground black pepper
3 ounces thinly sliced prosciutto
8 whole fresh sage leaves

About 4 tablespoons (1/2 stick) unsalted butter
About 2 tablespoons olive oil
1 cup dry white wine

SERVES 4

HERE IS AN alternative WAY TO ENJOY THIS FAVOR-ITE dish THAT IS MADE WITH CHICKEN instead OF VEAL.

✳ Rinse chicken breasts under cold water and pat dry with paper towels. Trim away the tendons and any connective tissue or fat from the breasts. Separate the little fillet from each breast and reserve for another use.

✳ Place each chicken breast between 2 sheets of waxed paper or plastic wrap and pound with mallet or other flat, heavy instrument to a uniform thickness of about 1/8 inch. Lightly sprinkle the chicken with salt and pepper.

✳ Trim the prosciutto slices to fit precisely on top of chicken breasts. Top each chicken piece with a slice of prosciutto and 1 or 2 sage leaves, securing each leaf in place with a toothpick.

✳ In a heavy-bottomed sauté pan or skillet (without a nonstick coating), combine 2 table-spoons butter and 2 tablespoons olive oil over medium-high heat. When the butter stops foaming, add as many of the chicken pieces as will fit comfortably without crowding the pan. Brown on one side, turn, and cook on the other side until browned and opaque all the way through, 4 to 5 minutes total. Use a small, sharp knife to check doneness. Trans-fer the chicken to a warmed plate and cover to keep warm. Cook the remaining chicken in the same way, adding a little more butter and oil if necessary to prevent sticking.

✳ When all the chicken is cooked, discard the cooking fat from the pan. Return the pan to medium-high heat. Add the white wine and salt and pepper to taste to the pan and scrape the bottom of the pan with a wooden spoon to loosen any browned bits. Reduce the wine by half, add the remaining 2 tablespoons of butter and stir until melted. Discard the toothpicks and transfer chicken breasts to 4 individual plates. Pour the sauce over the chicken and serve.

Stewed Chicken with Chipotles and Prunes

MARTHA ROSE SHULMAN

2 1/2 quarts water

2 to 3 large or 4 small dried chipotle chilies

1/4 cup salt for the chipotles, plus additional for the stew

1 medium onion, halved

1 (3-pound) chicken, skin removed and cut up into serving pieces

8 prunes, pitted

4 large cloves garlic, 2 minced and 2 peeled

2 pounds (8 medium or 4 large) tomatoes or 2 (28-ounce) cans, drained

2 black peppercorns, ground (a pinch)

1 clove, ground (a pinch)

1 tablespoon canola or olive oil

1 (3-inch) cinnamon stick

✳ Bring 2 cups water to a boil in a saucepan and add the chilies and 1/4 cup salt. Stir to dissolve the salt, remove from heat, and let the chilies soak for 3 hours or longer. Flip the chilies over from time to time or weight with a plate so they will soak evenly.

✳ Combine 1 onion half, the remaining water, the chicken, and 2 of the prunes in a large pot and bring to a simmer. Skim any foam that rises. Add 1 teaspoon salt and the minced garlic. Simmer for 15 minutes while you prepare the ingredients for the sauce.

✳ To roast the tomatoes and onion: Preheat the broiler. Line a baking sheet with foil and place the fresh whole tomatoes and the other onion half on it. (Do not attempt to roast canned tomatoes.) Place under the broiler, 2 to 3 inches from the heat. Turn after 2 to 3 minutes, when the tomatoes have charred on one side, and repeat on the other side. The onion will take longer. Turn it several times, until charred and softened, approximately 5 to 10 minutes. Remove from the heat and transfer to a bowl. When the tomatoes are cool enough to handle, peel and core. Set aside.

✳ To toast the garlic: Heat a heavy skillet over medium heat and toast the garlic in its skin, turning or shaking the pan often, until it smells toasty and is blackened in several places, approximately 10 minutes. Remove from the heat and peel.

✳ Strain 2 1/2 cups of the chicken stock through a cheesecloth-lined strainer into a measuring cup. Keep the chicken in the remaining stock while you cook the sauce.

✱ Place the roasted onion and tomatoes (or drained canned tomatoes) in a blender along with any juices that have accumulated in the bowl. Add the toasted garlic. Drain the chipotles and rinse thoroughly in several changes of water to rid them of the salt. Add to the blender along with the ground pepper and clove and the 2 prunes you simmered with the chicken. Blend until smooth. Strain into a bowl through a medium-mesh strainer.

✱ Heat the oil in a large heavy casserole or large nonstick skillet over medium-high heat and add a bit of the tomato purée. If it sizzles loudly, add the rest (wait a couple of minutes if it doesn't). Stir together for approximately 3 to 5 minutes, until the sauce thickens slightly, and stir in ½ cup of the strained stock and ½ teaspoon salt. Turn the heat to low and simmer, stirring often, for 20 minutes, until the sauce is fragrant and thick. Add the chicken pieces, the remaining prunes, the cinnamon, the remaining 2 cups of strained stock from the chicken, and more salt to taste. (Strain the remaining stock and freeze or use for cooking rice.) Stir together, cover partially, and simmer over medium-low heat for 30 minutes, stirring from time to time, or until the chicken is tender, but cooked through. Taste and adjust the salt.

✱ To serve the chicken, evenly spoon the chicken and some sauce over rice, if desired.

Chicken Jambalaya

SERVES 4

JAMBALAYA IS A POPULAR

DISH THROUGHOUT THE

AMERICAN South, BUT

IT IS MOST OFTEN ASSOCI-

ATED WITH THE COOKING

OF New Orleans.

2 tablespoons butter or vegetable oil
1 chicken (about 2¹/₂ pounds), cut into
   serving pieces, fat and excess skin
   trimmed
Salt and freshly ground black pepper
1 green bell pepper, cored, seeded,
   and diced
¹/₂ cup diced celery
1 cup long-grain white rice

¹/₂ teaspoon ground red pepper flakes
3 cups boiling water
¹/₄ cup chopped fresh parsley
¹/₄ teaspoon dried thyme
³/₄ teaspoon salt
¹/₈ teaspoon freshly ground black pepper
1 bay leaf
1 cup slivered cooked ham (about 1 ounce)
   or 1 chorizo sausage, thinly sliced

✳ Heat the butter or oil in a large skillet over medium heat. Add the chicken pieces and cook, turning frequently, until browned on all sides, about 10 minutes. Remove to a plate and season with salt and pepper to taste.

✳ To the drippings in the skillet used to cook chicken, add the green pepper, celery, rice, and red pepper flakes. Cook over medium-low heat, stirring to coat all the ingredients with the butter or oil.

✳ Add the boiling water, parsley, thyme, salt, pepper, and bay leaf. Return the chicken to the skillet and add the cooked ham or sausage. Cover the skillet and cook over medium-low heat until the water is absorbed and the chicken is cooked through, about 20 minutes. Remove cover and continue to cook until all excess moisture is evaporated, about 3 minutes. Serve hot.

Ivy's Cranberry-Orange Turkey Breast

LORA BRODY

1 fresh or defrosted uncooked turkey
   breast, skin on (approximately
   3 pounds)
Salt and freshly ground pepper
4 large onions, peeled, cut in half,
   and thinly sliced
4 large carrots, peeled and cut into
   1/2-inch slices

1 cup dried cranberries
1 cup dried apricots
6 ounces (3/4 cup) partially defrosted
   orange juice concentrate
10 to 12 ounces orange marmalade
2 cups chicken broth (or white wine)
2 teaspoons salt
Freshly ground pepper

✳ Preheat the oven to 325°F.

✳ Rinse the turkey and pat dry. Place the breast in a Dutch oven or roasting pan and sprinkle with salt and pepper. Place the onions, carrots, cranberries, and apricots around the turkey.

✳ In a bowl, combine the orange juice concentrate, marmalade, and broth and mix well. Pour the mixture over the vegetables and fruit in the pan. Add a little water, if necessary, to make sure there are at least 2 inches of liquid in the bottom of the pan. Cover and cook for approximately 2 hours, or until the internal temperature registers 170°F. Let rest for 10 minutes.

✳ To serve, slice with an electric knife. The turkey is very good served with rice or over noodles.

SERVES 6

LORA BRODY, CREATOR OF THIS ONE-POT DISH, THINKS IT'S PERFECT FOR THE novice COOK, BUT EVEN EXPERIENCED COOKS WILL APPRECIATE ITS simplicity AND COLOR. USE YOUR FAVORITE dried fruits AS SUBSTITUTES FOR THE CRANBERRIES AND APRICOTS; APRICOT PRESERVES CAN BE USED instead OF ORANGE MARMALADE.

Grilled Quail

CHRIS JOHNSON

6 whole quail
Salt and freshly ground pepper
6 jumbo or 18 medium shrimp, peeled
  and deveined
2 teaspoons turmeric
2 teaspoons dry mustard
1 tablespoon vegetable oil

16 baby carrots, trimmed and peeled
  (other seasonal vegetables of your
  choice can be substituted)
1 cup whipping cream
½ cup dark veal stock (available at
  specialty shops)
3 cups cooked wild rice

✶ Season quail with salt and pepper, inside and out. Season shrimp with salt and pepper. Mix together turmeric, dry mustard, and oil into a paste and rub into shrimp. Cover and refrigerate both quail and shrimp for 1 hour.

✶ Start a fire or turn gas grill to medium.

✶ Bring water to a boil in a pot with a steamer rack. Add carrots, cover, and steam until carrots are tender. Remove carrots from pot and keep warm while cooking quail and shrimp.

✶ When coals are covered with gray ash and there is a gentle red glow underneath, place quail on grill. Cook for 4 minutes and turn. At this point, place shrimp on grill. After 2 minutes, turn shrimp. After 2 more minutes, remove both quail and shrimp.

✶ While quail and shrimp are cooking on grill, place cream and veal stock in a medium saucepan and simmer, whisking ingredients together. Simmer until reduced by about one-third, about 4 minutes, until thickened and sauce-like. Keep warm.

✶ Place ½ cup of cooked wild rice on a large soup plate. Place 1 quail and 1 large shrimp (or 3 medium shrimp) on each bed of rice. Arrange 4 carrots artfully on each plate. Spoon sauce over the dish and serve immediately.

Cornish Hen Under a Brick

ROZANNE GOLD

1½-pound Cornish hen
Salt and freshly ground black pepper
3 tablespoons Garlic Oil (see below),
    plus additional for drizzling, if desired

½ cup dry white wine
1 tablespoon chopped fresh rosemary

✳ With kitchen shears, cut the hen along the length of the backbone. With your fist, pound the bird flat so that it is butterflied. Season with salt and pepper.

✳ Heat the oil in a large nonstick skillet. Place the hen, skin side down, in the oil and place a brick wrapped in aluminum foil on top. Cook over medium heat, turning every 2 to 3 minutes, replacing brick each time, for 10 to 12 minutes, or until golden brown. Remove hen to a large warm plate and keep warm.

✳ Add the wine and rosemary to the pan and reduce over high heat, scraping up the browned bits in the pan. When the sauce has thickened, pour it over the hen. Serve immediately. Drizzle with additional garlic oil, if desired.

Garlic Oil

16 medium cloves garlic
2 cups olive oil

2 California bay leaves
½ teaspoon whole black peppercorns

✳ Peel the garlic and place with oil in a small, heavy pot. Heat gently for 5 minutes, or until bubbles form on top. Remove from heat and add bay leaves and peppercorns. Let steep and cool. The garlic oil will last 2 weeks in the refrigerator. *Makes 2 cups.*

SERVES 1 OR 2

YOU REALLY NEED A BRICK FOR MAKING THIS DISH, BECAUSE THE authentic ITALIAN PREPARATION REQUIRES THAT THE HEN LIE COMPLETELY FLAT WHILE cooking. YOU WILL BE REWARDED FOR YOUR efforts WITH ULTRA-CRISP SKIN AND succulent MEAT.

Pan-Seared Salmon with Orange-Basil Pesto

SOREN C. FAKSTORP

SERVES 4

THIS colorful RECIPE IS MEANT FOR THE GLORY DAYS OF SUMMER, WHEN BASIL AND heirloom tomatoes ARE AT THEIR PEAK.

Orange Basil Pesto Sauce
4 whole oranges, peeled
2 shallots, peeled and diced
1/2 cup tightly packed basil leaves
1/4 cup balsamic vinegar
1 cup extra-virgin olive oil

6 to 8 tomatoes, different colors of
    heirloom varieties, if available, sliced
Juice of 2 lemons
1/2 cup olive oil
Salt and freshly ground black pepper

Onion Rings
Vegetable oil for deep-frying
2 red onions, peeled and thinly sliced
Flour for dredging

2 tablespoons vegetable oil (if using
    a nonstick pan, no oil is needed)
4 (5-ounce) boneless salmon fillets
Salt and freshly ground black pepper

✱ To make orange-basil pesto, place oranges, shallots, and basil in a blender or bowl of a food processor. Blend or process until smooth. Add vinegar and blend until smooth again. With machine running, add olive oil in a thin stream to create a smooth emulsion. The pesto can be made up to a day in advance and refrigerated. (Bring pesto to room temperature before using.)

✱ Shortly before serving, arrange sliced tomatoes in overlapping concentric circles on a dinner plate. Drizzle with lemon juice and olive oil. Season with salt and pepper and set aside at room temperature.

✱ To make onion rings, pour 1 inch of vegetable oil into a deep, medium-size skillet. Heat oil until a drop of water slides along surface of oil. While oil is heating, dredge onion rings in flour. Fry onion rings in hot oil until golden and crispy, 1 to 2 minutes. Keep onion rings warm while cooking salmon.

✱ In a large sauté pan, add the 2 tablespoons of vegetable oil. Season salmon fillets with salt and pepper, place in warm oil, and pan-fry until golden brown, 2 to 3 minutes per side.

✱ Place salmon fillets on top of tomatoes on serving plates. Spoon pesto on fish and top with onion rings. Serve immediately.

Cedar-Planked Salmon

MARGARET CHISHOLM

1 plank of cedar (see note), approximately
    18 inches long x 8 inches wide
3 tablespoons olive oil

1 (2-pound) side of salmon
Coarse sea salt
Freshly ground pepper

✳ Preheat the oven to 350°F. Very lightly brush the plank with a bit of the oil. Place the plank in the oven until it begins to brown slightly and becomes warm, approximately 10 to 15 minutes.

✳ Meanwhile, remove the skin from the salmon and, using tweezers, pluck out the small pin bones. Brush the salmon with the remaining oil. Season both sides with salt and pepper.

✳ Remove the heated plank from the oven. Place the salmon on the plank, place the plank back into the oven, and roast the fish for 15 to 20 minutes, or until barely done in the thickest part. Serve immediately.

NOTE: Cedar planks are available at the lumber yard or through mail order—check the listing in the back of cooking magazines for a supplier. Just be sure the wood has not been chemically treated.

SERVES 4

LEADING VANCOUVER chef MARGARET CHISHOLM BROUGHT US THIS RECIPE, WHICH uses AN OLD NATIVE AMERICAN TECHNIQUE OF COOKING FISH ON A CEDAR plank THAT INFUSES IT WITH WONDERFUL FLAVOR. FOR convenience, ASK YOUR FISHMONGER TO REMOVE THE SKIN AND BONES FOR YOU.

Marinated Shrimp with
Soft Polenta and Asparagus

Marinade

$^1/_2$ serrano chili, seeded

2 cloves garlic, minced, plus $^1/_4$ teaspoon
    oil, or 1 teaspoon prepared minced
    garlic *(see page 13)*

$^1/_2$ cup dry sherry or dry white wine

$^1/_4$ cup olive oil

$^1/_4$ cup cider vinegar or rice vinegar

$^1/_4$ cup chopped onion

1 teaspoon chili powder

$^1/_2$ teaspoon salt

$1^1/_2$ pounds (30 to 40 medium) shrimp,
    peeled and deveined if necessary

Polenta

7 cups water

$1^1/_2$ teaspoons salt

4 cloves garlic, minced, plus $^1/_2$ teaspoon
    oil, or 2 teaspoons prepared minced
    garlic *(see page 13)*

2 cups yellow or white coarse cornmeal

2 large tomatoes, peeled, seeded, and cut
    into 1-inch wedges

18 ounces asparagus tips, cut on the bias
    into 3-inch-long pieces

1 tablespoon unsalted butter

$^1/_2$ cup grated Parmesan cheese

2 tablespoons chopped fresh cilantro

SERVES 6

DON'T BE fooled BY THE NUMBER OF INGREDIENTS. THIS DISH IS ACTUALLY QUITE easy AND THE RESULTS ARE WELL worth IT. YOU MAY ALSO SERVE THE POLENTA HARD AND CUT INTO TRIANGLES (SEE PHOTOGRAPH).

✱ Place all the marinade ingredients in a food processor fitted with the metal blade and process until smooth.

✱ Place the shrimp in a large bowl and pour the marinade over them, tossing to coat well. Place the shrimp in the refrigerator to marinate for 20 minutes.

✱ While the shrimp are marinating, make the polenta: Preheat the oven to 325°F. Bring the water, salt, and garlic to a boil in an ovenproof sauce pot. Slowly whisk in the cornmeal in a slow, steady stream. Bring to boil, cover with a tight-fitting lid, and then place the pot in the oven to finish cooking for 20 minutes, or until the polenta is thick and creamy. Remove from the oven and keep warm.

✱ Preheat the oven to 325°F. With a slotted spoon, remove the shrimp from the marinade, shaking off any excess, and place on baking sheet. Bake for approximately 6 to 8 minutes, or until the shrimp turn pink and are firm to the touch but not tough.

✱ Pour the reserved marinade into a saucepan, add the tomato wedges, and simmer over low heat for 5 minutes. Set aside.

✱ Just before serving, steam the asparagus until al dente, approximately 3 to 5 minutes. Stir the butter, cheese, and cilantro into the polenta.

✱ To serve, place approximately 1 cup polenta in the center of each plate. Arrange the asparagus, shrimp, and tomato around the polenta and pour the sauce around the edges.

New England-Style Pot-au-Feu

SERVES 6

AN UPDATED, seafood VERSION OF THE TRADITIONAL FAMILY-STYLE BOILED DINNER, THIS IS one-pot COOKING AT ITS BEST.

3 cloves garlic, cut into slivers
2 tablespoons olive oil
1 onion, thinly sliced
1 cup thinly sliced celery
1 cup thinly sliced fennel
1 cup thinly sliced carrots
1 cup thinly sliced leeks (white parts only)
1/2 cup green peas
3 cups chicken stock (homemade or low-sodium canned), or clam juice

10 ounces (6 small) Yukon Gold potatoes, quartered
1 cup white wine
1 tablespoon fresh thyme leaves, stems removed, plus 6 additional thyme sprigs for garnish
2 large tomatoes, peeled, seeded, and juice removed (flesh only)
8 ounces quality crab meat such as snow crab, king crab, or stone crab

✳ In a large stock pot or Dutch oven, sauté the garlic in oil over low heat until aromatic, approximately 1 to 2 minutes. Add the onion, celery, fennel, carrots, leeks, peas, chicken stock, potatoes, wine, and thyme and simmer until the vegetables are tender, but not mushy, approximately 20 minutes.

✳ Place the tomatoes and the crab lumps on top of the vegetables and simmer for another 2 minutes to warm the crab. (Do not overcook the crab.)

✳ To serve, spoon the stew into large bowls and garnish with fresh thyme sprigs.

BEEF, PORK, AND LAMB

Beef Daube with Dried Cèpes

GEORGEANNE BRENNAN

4 pounds boneless beef chuck roast or
  a combination of boneless chuck and
  beef shank
2 yellow onions
3 carrots
8 fresh thyme branches, each about
  6 inches long
2 bay leaves
1 fresh rosemary branch, about 6 inches
  long
2 teaspoons salt
2 tablespoons freshly ground black pepper
4 cloves garlic

1 orange zest strip, 4 inches long and
  1/2 inch wide
1 bottle (750 ml) dry red wine such as
  Côtes du Rhône, Zinfandel, or Burgundy
1/3 cup minced roulade (peppered
  pancetta) or salt pork
2 tablespoons all-purpose flour
1 cup water
2 ounces dried cèpes, some broken into
  2 or 3 pieces, others left whole
1 pound wide, flat dried pasta noodles
1/2 to 3/4 cup grated Parmesan cheese
1/2 cup chopped fresh flat-leaf parsley

✱ Cut the beef chuck into 2- to 2½-inch squares. Trim off and discard any large pieces of fat. If using beef shank, cut the meat from the bone in pieces as large as possible. Place the meat in a large enamel, glass, earthenware, or other nonreactive bowl.

✱ Quarter one of the onions, and add the pieces to the meat along with the carrots, thyme, bay leaves, rosemary, one teaspoon of salt, one tablespoon of the pepper, 2 cloves of the garlic, and the orange zest. Pour the wine over all and turn to mix and immerse the ingredients. Cover and marinate in the refrigerator for at least 4 hours, or as long as overnight.

✱ To cook the daube, put the roulade or salt pork in a heavy-bottomed casserole or a Dutch oven large enough to hold the marinating mixture. Place over medium-low heat and cook, stirring occasionally until the fat is released, about 5 minutes. Discard the crisped bits of roulade or salt pork.

✱ Dice the remaining onion and mince the remaining 2 garlic cloves, and add to the fat. Sauté over medium heat until translucent, 3 to 5 minutes. Remove with a slotted spoon and set aside.

✱ Drain the meat and reserve the marinade. Pat the meat as dry as possible. Do not be concerned by the meat's purplish color, as this is caused by the wine. Add the meat to the pot a few pieces at a time and sauté for about 5 minutes, turning them once or twice. The meat will darken in color, but will not truly "brown."

(continued on next page)

SERVES 6 TO 8

DAUBES REQUIRE THE LESS tender CUTS OF BEEF, WHICH HAVE GELATINOUS SINEWS AND TENDONS THAT thicken AND flavor THE SAUCE. GEORGEANNE BRENNAN STARTS THIS AT LEAST A DAY IN ADVANCE, SO THAT THE MEAT CAN marinate OVERNIGHT. THE MEAT IS SIMMERED THE NEXT DAY, AND CAN EASILY WAIT, ITS FLAVORS EVER deepening, FOR THE DAY AFTER IT IS COOKED TO BE SERVED. DRIED cèpes ARE MORE LIKELY TO BE LABELED UNDER THEIR ITALIAN NAME, *porcini*, IN THE UNITED STATES.

✳ Remove the pieces with a slotted spoon and continue cooking until all the meat has been sautéed. When the last of the meat pieces has been removed, add the flour and cook until it browns, stirring often.

✳ Raise the heat to high and slowly pour in the reserved marinade and all of its ingredients. Deglaze the pan by scraping up any bits clinging to the bottom. Return the sautéed onion, garlic, meat, and any collected juices to the pan. Add the remaining teaspoon of salt and the remaining tablespoon of pepper, the water, and the mushrooms and bring to a boil. Reduce the heat to very low, cover with a tight-fitting lid, and simmer until the meat can be cut through with the edge of a spoon and the liquid has thickened, 2½ to 3 hours.

✳ Remove daube from heat. Discard the carrots, herb branches, and onion quarters. Skim off some, but not all, of the fat, as some is necessary to coat the pasta.

✳ Meanwhile, bring a large pot of salted water to a boil. Add the pasta, stir well, and cook until just tender. Drain.

✳ Put the pasta in a warmed serving bowl and ladle some of the sauce from the daube over it, adding more salt and pepper, if desired, and topping with ¼ cup of the Parmesan cheese and the parsley. Serve the daube directly from its cooking vessel, or from a serving bowl. Pass remaining cheese at the table.

Pork Loin Roast in a Port Wine Sauce with Roasted Potato Wedges and Sautéed Spinach

1 tablespoon oil, preferably canola
1 1/2 pounds boneless pork loin
1 1/2 pounds Red Bliss or Russet
    potatoes, cut in 3/4-inch wedges
Salt and freshly ground pepper
1 tablespoon chopped fresh thyme, or
    1 teaspoon dried thyme

Port Wine Sauce
1 large onion, thinly sliced
1 tablespoon brown sugar
1/4 cup currant jelly or red plum jelly
1 1/2 cups port wine
1/2 cup heavy cream

1 tablespoon vinegar, preferably cider
Salt and freshly ground pepper
4 cloves garlic, minced, plus 1/2 teaspoon
    oil, or 2 teaspoons prepared minced
    garlic (see page 13)
1 tablespoon olive oil
3 pounds fresh spinach, stems removed,
    washed, and drained (or 1 1/2 pounds
    frozen)
1/4 teaspoon nutmeg
1/2 teaspoon salt
1/4 teaspoon freshly ground pepper
1 tablespoon balsamic vinegar

SERVES 6

THIS IS A COMPLETE meal THAT COMES TOGETHER IN NO TIME. THE potatoes ARE COOKED ALONGSIDE THE PORK LOIN AND THE SPINACH CAN BE PREPARED WHILE THE roast IS RESTING.

✱ Preheat the oven to 350°F. In a large sauté pan, heat the oil, then add the pork and brown on all sides, approximately 10 to 15 minutes. Transfer the pork to a rack placed in a roasting pan and cook in the oven for 20 minutes.

✱ Season the potato wedges with salt, pepper, and thyme. Add the potatoes to the roasting pan and continue roasting for another 30 to 40 minutes, or until the potatoes are golden brown on both sides and the internal temperature of the roast reaches 150 to 165°F. Remove from the oven and let the roast rest.

✱ To make the port wine sauce, add the onion and brown sugar to the original sauté pan and cook over medium-low heat until they caramelize, approximately 10 minutes. Add the jelly and the port to the pan and simmer until the liquid reduces in volume by one half, approximately 10 to 12 minutes. Add the heavy cream and continue cooking over low heat until the sauce reduces by one third, and coats the back of a spoon. Stir in the vinegar and season with salt and pepper.

✱ In a large, deep pot with a tight-fitting lid, sauté the garlic in the olive oil over low heat until aromatic, approximately 1 to 2 minutes. Add the spinach, cover, and cook for approximately 2 minutes, or until wilted and turned bright green. Remove the pan from the heat, uncover, and stir in the nutmeg, salt, pepper, and vinegar.

✱ To serve, divide the spinach evenly and place to one side of each plate. Slice the pork on the bias into 1/4-inch-thick slices and fan 2 to 3 slices next to the spinach. Arrange the potatoes next to the pork and drizzle the sauce all over.

Pork Tenderloin with Molasses, Bacon, and Porcini Vinaigrette

MICHAEL CHIARELLO

Porcini Oil
1 ounce dried porcini mushrooms
1 cup olive oil

6 tablespoons porcini oil *(from above)* or good quality olive oil
2 pounds pork tenderloin
Salt and freshly ground pepper

1/2 pound bacon, cut into 1/4-inch dice
1 tablespoon finely chopped garlic
1 teaspoon finely chopped rosemary or 1/2 teaspoon dried rosemary
1/3 cup balsamic vinegar
2 tablespoons dark molasses
1 tablespoon finely chopped fresh flat-leaf parsley

✳ To make the porcini oil, place the mushrooms in a food processor fitted with a metal blade and chop until fine. Place in a pot with the oil and heat until the mixture begins to bubble. Let cook 10 to 15 seconds and remove from heat. Swirl until just warm. Strain into a bowl through 4 layers of cheesecloth. Squeeze well to extract as much oil as possible. Pour into a sterilized jar or bottle, seal tightly, refrigerate, and use within 1 week. *Makes approximately ¾ cup porcini oil.*

✳ Preheat the oven to 400°F. Heat 3 tablespoons of the porcini oil in a heavy, ovenproof pan over medium-high heat until hot. Season the pork with salt and pepper and then add to the pan and brown on all sides, approximately 3 to 5 minutes. Transfer the pan to the oven and roast until the internal temperature reaches 165°F, approximately 15 minutes.

✳ When the pork has cooked, transfer it to a rimmed platter and cover to keep warm. Pour the cooking juices from the pan over the meat. Return the pan to medium heat, add the bacon, and cook until crisp, approximately 8 to 10 minutes. Drain off and discard all but 2 tablespoons of fat from the pan. Add the garlic and sauté over medium-high heat until light brown. Add the rosemary, remove from the heat, add the vinegar, and stir up all the brown bits that have stuck to the bottom of the pan. Add the molasses and stir well.

✳ To finish the sauce, return the pan to the heat and stir in the meat juices that have accumulated around the meat. Add the parsley and remaining 3 tablespoons porcini oil. Cover to keep warm.

✳ To serve, slice the pork on the bias into ¼-inch-thick slices and fan 3 slices across each plate. Spoon the sauce over the meat.

Beer and Lamb Stew with
Potatoes and Onion Gravy

1 1/2 pounds lamb stew meat (such as
    shoulder), cut into large chunks
Salt and freshly ground pepper
1 tablespoon oil
1 1/2 pounds (approximately 5 medium)
    onions, thinly sliced
4 cloves garlic, minced, plus 1/2 teaspoon
    oil, or 2 teaspoons prepared minced
    garlic (see page 13)
1 (12-ounce) bottle dark beer, such as
    Samuel Adams Double Bock, or your
    favorite American microbrew

1/3 cup dark molasses or dark Karo syrup
2 bay leaves
2 large sprigs fresh thyme or 1 teaspoon
    dried thyme
1 sprig of fresh rosemary or 1 teaspoon
    dried rosemary
1 teaspoon salt
1 1/2 pounds (approximately 10 medium)
    red potatoes, cut into 1 1/2-inch dice
1/4 cup chopped fresh parsley, for
    garnish (optional)

SERVES 6

YOU CAN also PREPARE

THIS DISH USING BEEF

instead OF LAMB.

✳ Cut the lamb into 2-inch chunks and dry with paper towels. Season on all sides with salt and pepper.

✳ Place a large, nonstick, ovenproof roasting pan over medium high until very hot. Add the lamb chunks and sear, turning to brown all over. Remove from pan.

✳ Preheat the oven to 325°F. Add the oil, onions, and garlic to the pan and sauté over low heat until brown and caramelized, approximately 10 minutes. Increase the heat to medium, add the beer, and stir to scrape up any brown bits from the bottom of the pan. Cook for 2 to 3 minutes until the liquid is slightly reduced.

✳ Add the molasses, bay leaves, thyme, rosemary, and salt to the pan, place the lamb on top of the mixture, and add the potatoes. Cover and bake in the oven for 30 to 40 minutes, or until the lamb is tender when pierced with a fork.

✳ Remove the lamb and the potatoes from the pan and set aside on a rimmed plate. Bring the braising liquid to a boil and cook over medium-high heat for approximately 10 minutes, or until the sauce has thickened.

✳ To serve, place the potatoes on the bottom of an attractive serving dish, top with lamb chunks, and pour the onion gravy on top, partially covering the meat. Garnish with parsley, if desired.

Grilled Steak with Spicy Guajillo Sauce

RICK BAYLESS

SERVES 6

SMOKY, CHARCOALED BEEF LIT UP BY THE slow-simmered GUAJILLO SAUCE IS ONE OF THE CROWNING glories OF THE MEXICAN KITCHEN. THE SAUCE CAN BE MADE SEVERAL DAYS IN ADVANCE AND THE steaks CAN BE SLIPPED INTO THE MARINADE UP TO 4 HOURS BEFORE grilling.

Guajillo Sauce
6 cloves garlic, unpeeled
16 guajillo chilies, stemmed and seeded (about 4 ounces total)
1 teaspoon dried oregano, preferably Mexican
1/4 teaspoon black pepper, preferably freshly ground
1/8 teaspoon cumin, preferably freshly ground
3 2/3 cups beef broth, plus a little more if needed
2 1/2 tablespoons vegetable or olive oil
Salt, about 1 1/2 teaspoons, depending on the saltiness of the broth
Sugar, about 1 1/2 teaspoons

1 tablespoon cider vinegar
6 (6-ounce) beef steaks, such as tenderloin, New York strip, or sirloin, about 1 inch thick
1 large red onion, cut into 1/2-inch-thick slices
Several sprigs of cilantro, for garnish

✳ To make the guajillo sauce, roast the unpeeled garlic cloves directly on an ungreased griddle or heavy skillet over medium heat, turning occasionally, until soft (they'll blacken in spots), about 15 minutes; cool and peel.

✳ While the garlic is roasting, toast the chilies on another side of the griddle or skillet, 1 or 2 at a time, opening them flat and pressing them down hard onto the hot cooking surface with a spatula. When the chilies crackle, or even send up a wisp of smoke, flip and press down hard on the other side with the spatula.

✳ Place the cooked chilies in a small bowl with hot water and let rehydrate for 30 minutes, stirring frequently to ensure even soaking. Drain and discard the water.

✳ Combine the oregano, black pepper, and cumin in a food processor or blender, along with the garlic, drained chilies, and 2/3 cup of the broth. Blend to a smooth purée, scraping and stirring every few seconds. (If the mixture won't go through the blender blades, add a little more liquid.) Press through a medium-mesh sieve into a bowl.

✳ Heat 1½ tablespoons of the oil in a heavy, medium-size pot (such as a Dutch oven or Mexican *cazuela*) over medium-high heat. When the oil is hot enough to make a drop of the purée sizzle sharply, add the purée and stir constantly until it reduces to a thick paste, 5 to 7 minutes. Stir in the remaining 3 cups of broth, partially cover, and simmer over a medium-low heat, stirring occasionally, for about 45 minutes, until the flavors come together. If necessary, stir in a little broth to bring mixture to a medium, saucy consistency. Taste and season with about 1 teaspoon of the salt and the sugar.

✳ To marinate the steaks, mix ¼ cup of the sauce with the vinegar and the remaining ½ teaspoon of salt in a large bowl. Lay the steaks in marinade and turn to coat evenly. Let marinate, covered and refrigerated, while preparing the fire. (It is best not to let the steaks marinate for longer than 4 hours, because it will affect the color and texture of the meat.)

✳ Light a gas grill or prepare a charcoal fire, letting the coals burn until they are covered with gray ash and are medium-hot. Position the grill grate about 8 inches above the coals and lightly oil. Lay the steaks on the hottest portion of the grill and let them sear for 4 to 5 minutes on one side, then turn and finish on the other side (4 to 5 minutes more for medium-rare).

✳ While the steaks are cooking, separate the onion into rings and toss them with the remaining 1 tablespoon of oil. Spread them on the grill around the steaks and cook, stirring and turning with tongs or a spatula, until lightly browned and crisp-tender, 6 to 8 minutes.

✳ As the steaks and onion are done, heat the sauce to a simmer. Serve the steaks as soon as they come off the grill with a generous serving of the sauce and a topping of the onions. Garnish with sprigs of cilantro.

VARIATIONS: Anything tender enough to be grillable can be used in this dish, from beef steaks, to pork chops and tenderloin, to chicken, duck, and quail, to shrimp, scallops, and fish steaks, to vegetables like sweet potato, zucchini, and eggplant.

SIDE DISHES

Acorn Squash with Maple Syrup

1 large acorn squash, cut in half, seeds
   removed, and cut into 6 wedges
1/4 cup maple syrup
1/4 cup dark rum

1/2 teaspoon cinnamon
2 tablespoons unsalted butter, melted
Pinch of salt

✱ Preheat the oven to 375°F. Lightly grease an ovenproof casserole dish. Place the acorn wedges, cut-side down, in the casserole.

✱ In a small bowl, mix the maple syrup, rum, and cinnamon together. Pour the mixture evenly over the squash.

✱ Bake the squash for 45 minutes. (After 30 minutes, flip the squash over and continue baking.) Add the butter and the salt to the pan and continue baking for an additional 30 minutes, basting the squash with the maple syrup mixture every 10 minutes to prevent it from drying out, until the squash can be easily pierced with a fork. Serve immediately.

SERVES 6

THIS simple ACCOMPA-
NIMENT IS HOME COOK-
ING AT ITS best.

Glazed Carrots with Grapes and Walnuts

1 large bunch carrots, peeled and sliced
   1/4 inch thick (approximately 6 cups)
1/4 cup unsalted butter
1 cup chicken stock (homemade or
   low-sodium canned) or water

3 tablespoons sugar
1 cup seedless red grapes,
   cut in half
1/2 cup chopped walnuts
Salt and freshly ground pepper

✱ In a wide sauté pan over high heat, combine the carrots, butter, stock or water, and sugar. Bring to a boil, then reduce the heat to medium low. Simmer, uncovered, until the carrots are tender and the pan juices are reduced to a syrupy glaze, approximately 8 to 10 minutes.

✱ Stir in the grapes and walnuts and season to taste with salt and freshly ground pepper. Serve immediately.

SERVES 6 TO 8

THE carrots AND THE
GRAPES CAN BE PREPARED
FOR cooking UP TO
8 HOURS IN ADVANCE.

Mashed Potatoes with Escarole, Bacon, and Roasted Garlic

SERVES 6

YOU WILL ONLY NEED half OF THE ROASTED GARLIC FOR THIS RECIPE, BUT IT IS EASIER TO ROAST AN ENTIRE head AND SAVE THE EXTRA garlic FOR ANOTHER USE.

1 head garlic
1 1/2 pounds (approximately 5 medium) Yukon Gold or Russet potatoes, peeled and cut into 1/2-inch dice
2 ounces (approximately 3 strips) bacon, cut into small dice

1 small head (approximately 4 cups) escarole or other dark green leaf, washed, dried, and cut into 2-inch pieces
1/4 teaspoon freshly ground pepper
1 1/4 cups low-fat milk, warmed
1/2 teaspoon salt

✳ Preheat the oven to 350°F. Slice just enough off the top of the garlic head so that the tips are exposed, then tightly wrap in foil, and roast for 40 minutes, or until golden brown and extremely soft. Squeeze the bulbs to remove the roasted cloves.

✳ In a large pot, place the potatoes and enough cold, salted water to cover the potatoes by 2 inches and bring to a boil; cook over medium heat for approximately 20 minutes, or until tender when pierced with a fork. Drain and set aside.

✳ In a large sauté pan, cook the bacon over medium-high heat until crisp, approximately 8 to 10 minutes. Remove the bacon and set aside. (For a lower fat version, remove the pan fat.) Either way, add the escarole and pepper to the pan, cover, and cook for 2 minutes, or just until wilted.

✳ In an electric mixer, mash the potatoes with the warm milk, half the roasted garlic, and salt. Fold in the escarole and crumble in the bacon. Serve immediately.

Home-Style Stuffed Artichokes

TOM LACALAMITA

4 large artichokes (approximately 8 to 10 ounces each), untrimmed

2 large eggs

1/4 cup Pecorino-Romano cheese

1 clove garlic, peeled and minced

1 tablespoon minced parsley

Pinch of freshly ground black pepper

1 cup water

1 teaspoon salt

1 bay leaf

2 tablespoons extra-virgin olive oil

✳ Remove the stems from the artichokes with a sharp knife. Tear off and discard the top 2 or 3 layers of tough outer leaves. Trim the base so that the artichokes stand flat. Cut off 1/2 to 1 inch from the tops of the artichokes. Carefully open the center of the artichoke to expose the center leaves and choke. Pull out and remove any thorny leaves, which are usually tinged with purple. With a teaspoon, scoop out and discard any fuzzy matter from the center choke. Set aside.

✳ To prepare the filling, beat together the eggs, cheese, garlic, parsley, and black pepper in a large bowl. Set aside.

✳ Pour the water into the pressure cooker. Add the salt and stir to mix. Add the bay leaf. Carefully open up the artichoke leaves slightly, starting from the center and working outward, taking care not to break the leaves. Place the prepared artichokes in the pressure cooker standing up. Drizzle an equal amount of the egg mixture over the artichokes, being certain to spoon some into the center. Drizzle with olive oil.

✳ Position the pressure cooker lid and lock into place. Place over high heat and bring to high pressure. Adjust the heat to stabilize the pressure and cook 7 minutes. Remove from heat and lower pressure using the cold-water release method. Open the pressure cooker. Carefully remove the artichokes using a slotted spoon and place in individual serving bowls. Spoon a couple of tablespoons of the cooking liquid over each artichoke before serving.

NOTE: **The Cold-Water Release Method.** When using a pressure cooker, you will most often want to release the pressure and stop the cooking process as quickly as possible. The best way to do this is to carefully place pressure cooker in sink and run cold water over the lid. You will normally hear a decompressing sound—almost like a swooshing "pop"— once all the pressure has been released.

SERVES 4

ITALIANS LOVE TO stuff THEIR VEGETABLES. THIS IS AN impressive SIDE DISH, MADE EASY BY THE PRESSURE COOKER.

Eggplant Stuffed with Onions and Kefalotiri

DIANE KOCHILAS

8 medium-size eggplants (about 1/2 pound each)
1/2 cup olive oil
Salt and freshly ground black pepper
8 small onions, peeled and coarsely chopped (about 6 cups)
4 to 6 cloves garlic, chopped
3 large ripe tomatoes (about 2 pounds), cored, peeled, and coarsely chopped
1 cup coarsely chopped fresh parsley
1/2 pound Greek kefalotiri cut into 1-inch cubes, plus 1/2 cup grated

✳ Leaving the stems on the eggplants, and using a small paring knife, hold each eggplant horizontally and cut through the skin, scooping away about one-third of its flesh from the center. Discard the flesh, or reserve for some other use. Heat 4 to 6 tablespoons of the olive oil in a large skillet and sauté the eggplant until lightly browned and wrinkled. Remove from skillet and place in a lightly oiled baking pan and season with salt and pepper.

✳ Wipe skillet dry. Heat 2 to 3 more tablespoons of olive oil in the skillet and cook the onions for 5 to 6 minutes, until they just start to become transparent. Add the garlic and tomatoes, season with salt and pepper to taste, and simmer, uncovered, for 5 to 8 minutes. Remove from heat, toss in the parsley, and cool slightly. Preheat the oven to 375°F.

✳ Place about 4 cubes of cheese in the belly of each eggplant and fill each eggplant generously with the onions and tomatoes so that they form a mound over the opening. Sprinkle with a little grated cheese. Bake for about 25 minutes, or until eggplants are tender and the cheese is melted. Serve warm.

Eggplant Casserole

SERVES 6

Filling

3 cups chicken stock (homemade or
   low-sodium canned)
1 cup (7 ounces) dry barley
8 ounces part-skim mozzarella cheese, cut
   into small dice (approximately 2 cups)
4 ounces Parmesan cheese, grated
   (approximately 1 cup)

Eggplant

2 pounds (approximately 1 medium)
   eggplant, unpeeled, cut into $1/4$-inch-
   thick slices
2 tablespoons olive oil

Tomato Sauce

4 cloves garlic, minced, plus $1/2$ teaspoon
   oil, or 2 teaspoons prepared minced
   garlic (see page 13)
1 tablespoon olive oil
1 medium onion, thinly sliced
   (approximately 1 cup)
1 (16-ounce) can diced or crushed tomatoes
1 tablespoon tomato paste
1 bay leaf
1 teaspoon fresh rosemary, minced, or
   $1/4$ teaspoon dried rosemary
Pinch of sugar
Pinch of cayenne pepper

THIS meatless CASEROLE CAN BE PREPARED SEVERAL HOURS ahead OR THE DAY BEFORE, AND THEN BAKED OFF WHEN YOU ARE READY TO SERVE IT. IF YOU'RE PRESSED FOR time, YOU CAN USE A store-bought TOMATO SAUCE.

✻ To make the filling, in a medium pot bring the chicken stock to boil. Add the barley, cover, bring to boil again, then reduce the heat to low and simmer for 35 to 40 minutes. When the barley is done, fold in the cheeses and mix well.

✻ Meanwhile, prepare the eggplant. Prepare a grill or preheat the broiler. Brush the eggplant slices with the oil and grill or broil until golden on both sides, approximately 3 to 5 minutes on each side, or until the eggplant begins to soften and is slightly browned. Transfer to a plate and set aside.

✻ To make the tomato sauce, lightly sauté the garlic in the olive oil in a sauté pan over low heat for 1 to 2 minutes, or until aromatic. Add the onion and cook until translucent, approximately 3 to 5 minutes. Add the tomatoes, tomato paste, bay leaf, rosemary, sugar, and cayenne and continue to cook for 10 minutes. Remove the bay leaf and set the sauce aside.

✻ Preheat the oven to 350°F. Lightly grease a 9- x 12-inch casserole dish with vegetable oil.

✻ To assemble the casserole, arrange half of the eggplant slices evenly on the bottom of the dish. Spread half the filling over the eggplant, and cover with half the tomato sauce. Top with another layer of eggplant, spread the remaining filling on top, and cover with a final layer of tomato sauce.

✻ Place the casserole dish on a baking sheet and bake for 35 minutes, or until bubbly. Remove from the oven and allow to cool for 10 to 15 minutes before slicing.

Baked Dumplings, Roman Style

JAMES MCNAIR

5 cups milk
1 1/2 teaspoons salt, or to taste
1/2 teaspoon freshly ground black pepper,
　or to taste
1/8 teaspoon freshly grated nutmeg, or
　to taste
1 1/2 cups coarsely ground semolina flour,
　preferably imported from Italy

1/2 cup freshly grated Parmesan cheese,
　preferably Parmigiano-Reggiano
3 egg yolks, lightly beaten
3 tablespoons minced fresh sage, or
　1 tablespoon crumbled dried sage
2 tablespoons unsalted butter, melted
Softened unsalted butter for greasing
　baking sheet and dish and for dotting
　on top

✳ In a large, heavy-bottomed saucepan, combine the milk, salt, pepper, and nutmeg over medium heat. Bring the milk almost to a boil. Reduce the heat to the lowest possible setting, and gradually pour in the semolina in a thin, steady stream, stirring constantly with a wooden spoon or a wire whisk. The mixture will thicken quickly, but continue cooking and stirring, scraping the bottom of the pan, until the mixture forms a very thick mass that pulls away from the sides of the pan, about 15 minutes. Remove from heat.

✳ Quickly stir 1/4 cup of the Parmesan cheese, the egg yolks, sage, and the melted butter into the hot semolina mixture, stirring well.

✳ Grease a large, shallow baking sheet with softened butter. Using a metal spatula dipped in cold water from time to time, spread the thick semolina mixture into a layer about 1/4 inch thick. Let cool to room temperature, then cover and refrigerate until the mixture is cold and firm, about 1 hour.

✳ Preheat oven to 400°F. Grease a 9 x 13-inch baking dish with softened butter and set aside.

✳ Using a biscuit cutter or straight-sided glass about 1 1/2 to 2 inches in diameter, cut the semolina sheet into rounds, dipping the cutter into cold water between cuts. Place the dumplings in the prepared baking dish, arranging them in slightly overlapping rows to form a single layer. Dot with softened butter and sprinkle in the remaining 1/4 cup Parmesan cheese.

✳ Place in the preheated oven and bake until golden and crusty, about 20 minutes. Remove from oven and let stand about 5 minutes before serving directly from the baking dish.

Savory Bread Pudding Layered with Asparagus, Fontina, and Mixed Spring Herbs

GEORGEANNE BRENNAN

12 to 16 thick slices of dry bread	1/2 cup chopped fresh herbs, such as
2 1/2 to 3 cups milk	chives, parsley, tarragon, sage,
1 pound asparagus	or thyme
3 eggs	1/4 cup freshly grated Romano cheese
1 teaspoon salt	4 ounces fontina cheese, slivered
1 teaspoon freshly ground black pepper	4 ounces Swiss cheese, slivered
	1 tablespoon butter, cut into small pieces

✳ Place the bread in a single layer in a shallow baking dish. Pour 2½ cups of the milk over the top. Let soak until the bread has absorbed the milk and becomes soft, about 30 minutes. Press the bread slices to extract the milk. Measure the milk; you should have ½ cup milk left after squeezing the bread. If not, make up the difference with the additional ½ cup milk as needed. Set the milk and bread aside.

✳ While the bread is soaking, trim the asparagus, removing the woody ends. Cut the stalks on the diagonal into thin slivers each about 2 inches long and ⅜ inch thick. Arrange the slivered asparagus on a steamer rack and place over gently boiling water. Cover and steam until barely tender, 2 to 3 minutes. Immediately place the asparagus under cold running water until cold. Drain and set aside.

✳ Preheat the oven to 350°F. Butter a 3-quart mold. (A soufflé dish works well.)

✳ In a medium bowl beat together the eggs, salt, pepper, and the ½ cup milk until well blended. Layer one-third of the bread in the prepared dish. Set 6 to 8 asparagus slivers aside and top the bread layer with half of the remaining asparagus and half of the mixed herbs. Strew one-third of each of the cheeses over the asparagus. Repeat the layers, using half of the remaining bread, all of the remaining asparagus and herbs, and half of the remaining cheese. Arrange the remaining bread on top, strew the remaining cheese over it, and garnish with the reserved asparagus slivers. Pour the egg mixture over the layers and then dot with butter.

✳ Bake in the preheated oven until the top is crusty brown and a knife inserted in the middle of the pudding comes out clean, about 45 minutes.

SERVES 6 TO 8

SAVE leftover BREAD FOR A WEEK OR SO, ESPECIALLY THE ENDS AND slices FROM BAGUETTES AND ANY PIECES FROM SPECIALTY BREADS SUCH AS FOCACCIA. LET THEM GET good AND DRY.

Polenta Casserole with Mushroom Sauce

SERVES 6

THE method OF

MAKING POLENTA

REVEALED IN THIS RECIPE

ELIMINATES THE need

TO STIR IT CONSTANTLY.

FOR A fancier

PRESENTATION, MAKE

INDIVIDUAL CASSEROLES

(SEE PHOTOGRAPH).

Polenta

6 cups water

1 teaspoon salt

2 cloves garlic, minced, plus $1/4$ teaspoon oil, or 1 teaspoon prepared minced garlic (see page 13)

2 cups coarse yellow cornmeal

Mushroom Sauce

1 ounce assorted dried mushrooms (such as porcini, chanterelles, or cèpes)

1 cup boiling water

2 cloves garlic, minced, plus $1/4$ teaspoon oil, or 1 teaspoon prepared minced garlic (see page 13)

2 tablespoons olive oil

1 onion, cut into small dice

1 pound white mushrooms, cut into $1/3$-inch slices

$1/2$ cup half-and-half

$1/4$ teaspoon freshly ground pepper

3 tablespoons chopped fresh parsley

1 cup grated pecorino cheese

1 cup grated mozzarella cheese

✳ To make the polenta, preheat the oven to 325°F. Bring the water, salt, and garlic to a boil in an ovenproof pot. Slowly whisk in the cornmeal in a steady stream. Bring to boil, cover with a tight-fitting lid, and then place the pot in the oven for 20 minutes to finish cooking or until thick and creamy.

✳ Pour the polenta onto a 12- x 18-inch lightly greased or nonstick baking sheet and spread evenly. Cover with plastic wrap and refrigerate for 40 minutes, or until cold.

✳ While the polenta is cooling, make the mushroom sauce: In a small bowl, soak the dried mushrooms in boiling water until soft, approximately 30 minutes. When soft, strain and reserve the soaking liquid.

✳ In a large sauté pan, sauté the garlic in the olive oil over medium-low heat until golden, approximately 1 to 2 minutes. Add the onion and continue sautéing until brown, approximately 5 minutes. Add the dried and fresh mushrooms and sauté for an additional 5 minutes. Add the half-and-half, pepper, and reserved mushroom water and cook over medium heat until the sauce is thickened and coats the back of a spoon. Remove from the heat and stir in the parsley.

✳ Preheat the oven to 375°F. To layer the casserole, cut the cooled polenta in half, width-wise. Lightly grease a 9- x 12-inch casserole dish. Line the bottom of the casserole dish with one of the polenta halves. Spread half of the mushroom sauce across the polenta. Mix together the cheeses and evenly distribute half on top. Place the second half of the polenta on top. Spoon the remaining mushroom sauce down the center of the polenta and sprinkle the entire casserole with the remaining cheese.

✳ Bake for 20 minutes, or until bubbly. Let cool for 15 minutes before serving.

Orange–Sweet Potato Hobo Pack

CHRIS SCHLESINGER AND JOHN WILLOUGHBY

Grillmaster CHRIS SCHLESINGER USES THE HEAT OF THE coals TO MAKE A FIRE-ROASTED version OF CANDIED SWEET POTATOES GUARAN- TEED TO WARM YOU UP IN autumn OR WINTER.

4 medium sweet potatoes, washed but not peeled, cut into rounds about 2 inches thick
1 orange, thinly sliced (including peel)
1 large red onion, peeled and quartered
1/3 cup raisins
1/4 cup olive oil

1/4 cup unsalted butter, cut into small bits
Salt and freshly ground black pepper to taste
1/3 cup fresh lemon juice (about 1 large lemon)
1/3 cup honey
1/3 cup roughly chopped parsley

✱ In a large bowl, combine the sweet potatoes, orange, onion, raisins, olive oil, and butter. Toss lightly, sprinkle with salt and pepper to taste, and toss lightly again.

✱ Start a fire in a grill.

✱ Lay out 2 sheets of heavy-duty foil, each about 2 feet long, one on top of the other. Place the sweet potato mixture in the center, then lay a third length of heavy-duty foil over the top. Fold the edges of the sheets together on all sides, closing the pack, continuing to roll until the sides come up against the food, forming a ridge around its perimeter. Place the pack right side up in the center of a fourth length of foil and fold the four sides over the top of the packet.

✱ The package is now ready for the coals. The fire should have passed its peak of intensity and be dying down, so that it consists primarily of glowing coals covered with a thin film of gray ash but very few flickering flames. Clear a place in the coals for the packet, leaving a thin layer of coals. Place the packet on the cleared area and heap up coals all around, but not directly on top. Cook, keeping watch and shifting the packet as needed, so it is continuously in contact with glowing coals, for 30 to 35 minutes, depending upon the intensity of the coals.

✱ While the hobo pack is cooking, combine the lemon juice, honey, and parsley in a small bowl and mix well to combine.

✱ Remove the foil packet from the coals, unroll the foil, drizzle the vegetables with the lemon-honey mixture, and serve at once.

Villager's Leek and Fennel Pie

DIANE KOCHILAS

Homemade Phyllo Dough

4 to 4^1/$_2$ cups all-purpose flour

1 scant teaspoon salt

1^1/$_2$ to 1^3/$_4$ cups warm water

^{1}/$_4$ cup olive oil

2 tablespoons red wine vinegar or strained
fresh lemon juice

NOTE: Make dough at least 2 hours
before assembling pie

Filling

^{1}/$_2$ cup extra-virgin olive oil, plus oil
for phyllo

2 large leeks, whites and green, trimmed,
washed, and coarsely chopped

2 medium fennel bulbs, trimmed, halved,
and coarsely chopped

1 cup chopped fresh dill

1 cup crumbled feta cheese

1 to 2 eggs

Salt and freshly ground black pepper

Grating (or pinch) of nutmeg

✳ To make homemade phyllo dough: Combine 4 cups of the flour and salt in a large mixing bowl and make a well in the center. Add the water, olive oil, and vinegar. Work the flour into the liquid with a fork, until a dough begins to form, then knead it in the bowl, adding a little more flour if necessary. The dough should be silky, pliant, and smooth. Cover and let rest at room temperature for at least 2 hours before using. (The dough can also be made in a stand mixer with a dough hook.)

✳ To make the filling, in a large skillet, heat 3 tablespoons of the olive oil. Add leeks and fennel and sauté over medium heat until pearly, about 7 minutes.

✳ In a large mixing bowl, combine the sautéed leeks and fennel with the dill, feta, remaining olive oil, and 1 egg. Mix well. If the mixture seems too dry, add the other egg. Season with salt, pepper, and nutmeg and toss again.

✳ Preheat oven to 350°F. With 1 teaspoon of olive oil, oil a 9 x 1-inch round baking dish. Divide the dough into 4 equal balls. Lightly flour a surface and roll out the first dough ball to a circle slightly larger than the circumference of the pan. Place the phyllo in the pan and oil it with 1 teaspoon of olive oil. Repeat with second dough ball. Spread the filling on top. Roll out the third ball of dough, oil it, and place it on top of the filling, and repeat with last ball. Pinch the bottom and top phyllo sheets together and roll inward to form the rim of the crust. Make two incisions with a sharp paring knife in the top of the dough. Bake for about 1 hour, or until the phyllo is golden. Remove, cool, and serve.

SERVES 6 TO 8

DIANE traveled EXTENSIVELY THROUGHOUT GREECE AND DISCOVERED MANY authentic AND DELICIOUS DISHES LIKE THIS ONE, WHICH IS PERFUMED WITH THE aromas OF FENNEL AND LEEK. YOU WILL also HAVE EXCELLENT RESULTS WITH frozen PHYLLO DOUGH.

Pacific Rim Risotto

3 cloves garlic

1 medium onion, quartered

1 tablespoon fresh ginger, peeled and minced

2 tablespoons olive oil

4 large boneless, skinless chicken breasts (about 1 pound total), each breast cut into 4 diagonal pieces

1 cup uncooked arborio rice

2 cups quartered white mushrooms, such as crimini

2 to 3 cups unsalted chicken broth

1/4 cup dry white wine or sherry

1 tablespoon sesame oil

1 teaspoon hot chile sauce

1/2 pound smoked linguiça (Portuguese) sausage (or other hot, smoked sausage), cut into 1 1/2-inch diagonal pieces

1/2 cup freshly grated Parmesan cheese

1/2 cup roasted cashews

1 cup unpacked cilantro leaves, for garnish

✴ In a food processor, finely chop garlic, onion, and ginger. Set aside.

✴ In a large, deep, heavy-bottomed skillet with a cover, heat olive oil. Add chicken breast pieces and cook over medium-high heat, until lightly golden and plump, about 3 minutes per side. Remove chicken from pan. Add onion mixture to skillet and sauté until translucent, 4 to 5 minutes.

✴ Add rice to pan and continue to sauté for 1 minute longer. Add mushrooms, 2 cups of the broth, wine or sherry, sesame oil, and chile sauce. Bring to a low simmer, cover, and simmer for 15 minutes (add more broth if mixture appears dry at this point).

✴ Gently place sausage pieces and chicken on top of rice mixture (do not mix in). Cover and continue to cook over medium heat for another 10 minutes.

✴ Fold in the cheese and place on a serving platter or in a shallow bowl. Sprinkle with cashews and cilantro. Serve immediately.

SERVES 6

CHUNKY bites OF CHICKEN AND SAUSAGE COMBINED WITH THE creamy RISOTTO MAKE THIS A WONDERFUL SIDE WHEN SERVED WITH A simple GREEN SALAD.

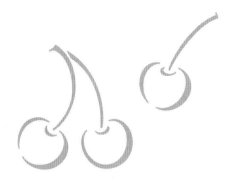

DESSERTS

Dee-lux Layered Choco-Oat Bars

Crust

1/3 cup unsalted butter or margarine, melted

1 1/2 cups graham cracker crumbs

Filling

12 ounces semisweet chocolate chips

1 cup butter or margarine, melted

2 cups firmly packed light brown sugar

1 tablespoon hot water

2 large eggs, lightly beaten

2 teaspoons vanilla extract

2 cups all-purpose flour

1/4 teaspoon baking soda

1 teaspoon baking powder

1 teaspoon salt

1 1/4 cups Quaker Quick Oats

1 cup chopped walnuts (see note below on toasting)

Chocolate Topping (optional)

6 ounces semisweet chocolate chips

MAKES 30 BARS

NINA SCHONDELMEIER FROM WEST HARTFORD, CONNECTICUT, TOOK FIRST **prize** FOR THIS DELECTABLE **treat**.

✱ To make the crust, preheat the oven to 350°F. Put the 1/3 cup of melted butter in the bottom of a 9 x 11-inch baking pan. Sprinkle the graham cracker crumbs on top and pat down firmly, covering the bottom of the pan and going 1/2 inch up the sides. Bake in oven for 10 minutes.

✱ To make the filling layers, immediately sprinkle the chocolate chips on top of the crumb crust after removing it from the oven. Let the chips melt, then spread the melted chocolate evenly over the entire crust.

✱ In a large bowl, mix the 1 cup of melted butter with the brown sugar and add the water. Add the eggs and vanilla. Mix well.

✱ In a separate bowl, sift together the flour, baking soda, baking powder, and salt. Stir the flour mixture into the creamed butter mixture. Add the oats and mix well. Stir the walnuts into the batter.

✱ Spread the batter in the pan over the melted chocolate chips and bake for 30 minutes, or until the sides pull away from the pan.

✱ If you choose to make the optional chocolate topping, immediately sprinkle the chocolate chips over the bar as soon as it comes out of the oven. Allow the chips to melt. Spread the melted chocolate over the bar. Allow the bar to cool in the pan on a wire rack for at least 1 hour before cutting into squares.

NOTE: For extra nutty flavor, spread the nuts on a cookie sheet and toast them in a preheated 350°F oven for 10 to 15 minutes, shaking pan occasionally to prevent nuts from burning.

Deep-Dish Pizza Cookie

MARCEL DESAULNIERS

White Chocolate Pizza Crust

3 cups all-purpose flour
1 teaspoon baking powder
1/2 teaspoon salt
4 ounces white chocolate, chopped into
    1/4-inch pieces
4 tablespoons granulated sugar
2 large egg yolks
1 teaspoon pure vanilla extract
12 ounces chilled unsalted butter, cut into
    1-ounce pieces

Pizza Topping

1 cup pecans
1 cup heavy cream
1/4 cup tightly packed light brown sugar
2 cups dried cranberries
4 ounces finely diced dried apricots
4 ounces semisweet chocolate, chopped
    into 1/4-inch pieces
2 ounces white chocolate, chopped into
    1/4-inch pieces

✳ To make the white chocolate pizza crust, preheat oven to 375°F. In a sifter combine the flour, baking powder, and salt. Sift onto a large piece of wax paper and set aside.

✳ Heat 1 inch of water in the bottom of a double boiler over medium heat. With the heat on, place the 4 ounces of white chocolate in the top half of the double boiler. Use a rubber spatula to stir the chocolate until completely melted and smooth, about 4 minutes. Transfer to a small bowl.

✳ In a large bowl whisk together the granulated sugar, egg yolks, and vanilla extract until combined and the sugar has dissolved. Add the melted white chocolate and whisk to combine. Set aside.

✳ Place the sifted dry ingredients and butter in the bowl of a stand mixer fitted with a paddle. Mix on low for 2 minutes, until the butter is cut into the flour and the mixture develops a coarse, mealy texture. Add the white chocolate mixture to the flour and butter mixture and mix on low for 30 seconds until a loose dough is formed.

✳ Transfer the dough to a clean, dry work surface and knead gently to form a smooth dough. Place the dough in a 9 x 3-inch springform pan and use your fingers to press the dough into the bottom and then three-quarters of the way up the sides of the pan. Place the pan on the center rack of the preheated oven and bake for 14 minutes. Remove the pan from the oven and allow to stand at room temperature while preparing the toppings.

(continued on page 160)

✳ To prepare the pizza cookie topping, toast the pecans on a baking sheet in the preheated oven for 5 minutes. Remove the pecans from the oven and cool to room temperature before chopping into ¼-inch pieces.

✳ Heat the heavy cream and light brown sugar in a large saucepan over medium heat. When hot, stir to dissolve the sugar. Bring to a boil, adjust the heat, and allow to simmer for 6 minutes until slightly thickened. Remove from heat and add the dried cranberries, apricots, and toasted pecans; stir with a rubber spatula to combine.

✳ Pour the topping onto the cooled crust, using a rubber spatula to spread topping evenly over crust. Sprinkle the chopped semisweet chocolate evenly over the entire surface of the topping.

✳ Place the pan on the center rack of the preheated oven and bake for 30 minutes until lightly browned around the edges. Remove the pizza from the oven and allow to cool to room temperature for 1 hour.

✳ While the pizza is cooling, again heat 1 inch of water in the bottom half of a double boiler over medium heat. With the heat on, place the 2 ounces of white chocolate in the top half of the double boiler. Use a rubber spatula to stir the chocolate until completely melted and smooth, about 3 minutes. Using a teaspoon, drizzle thin lines of white chocolate over the entire surface of the pizza topping. Allow the chocolate to become firm at room temperature before cutting.

✳ Remove the pizza from the pan and place on a cutting board. Using a serrated knife, cut the pizza into 12 to 16 slices. Store the pizza cookies in a tightly sealed plastic container until ready to serve.

Chocolate Chip Biscotti

$^1/_4$ cup vegetable oil
1 $^1/_2$ cups tightly packed brown sugar
2 eggs
1 teaspoon instant coffee diluted in
$^1/_4$ cup hot water
1 teaspoon vanilla extract
2 $^1/_2$ cups all-purpose flour

1 cup old-fashioned rolled oats, finely
ground in food processor or coffee
grinder
1 $^1/_2$ teaspoons baking powder
$^1/_2$ teaspoon salt
$^1/_2$ cup blanched slivered almonds, toasted
$^3/_4$ cup chocolate chips

✳ Preheat the oven to 375°F. Lightly grease a nonstick baking sheet.

✳ In a bowl, using an electric mixer, blend the oil, brown sugar, eggs, coffee, and vanilla extract together.

✳ In a separate bowl, mix together the flour, ground oats, baking powder, and salt. Add the flour mixture to the wet mixture, mixing until smooth. Using a wooden spoon, fold in the nuts and chocolate chips.

✳ Lightly flour your hands, divide the dough into 2 equal parts and shape each part into 2 logs, approximately 2 inches in diameter. Place the logs on the baking sheet, spacing them well apart, and bake in the oven for 25 minutes, or until firm to the touch. Let cool for 10 minutes. Leave the oven set at 350°F.

✳ Using a spatula, carefully transfer the logs to a work surface. Using a serrated knife, cut on the diagonal into slices $^1/_2$ inch thick. Return the slices cut-side down to the baking sheet. Bake until brown, approximately 20 minutes, or until the biscotti are dry and crisp.

✳ Transfer the cookies to wire racks to cool. Store in an airtight container at room temperature for up to 2 weeks.

MAKES APPROXIMATELY 3 DOZEN COOKIES

IN THESE BISCOTTI THE **nutty** FLAVORS OF CHOCOLATE, ROLLED OATS, AND **almonds** ARE COMBINED. FOR A **variation**, OMIT THE CHOCOLATE CHIPS AND ADD ¼ CUP OF COCOA POWDER AND 6 OUNCES OF **chocolate-covered** RAISINS.

Road Trip Cookies

MARCEL DESAULNIERS

2¹/₂ cups all-purpose flour
1 teaspoon baking soda
¹/₂ teaspoon salt
6 ounces semisweet chocolate, chopped
    into ¹/₄-inch pieces
³/₄ cup granulated sugar

³/₄ cup tightly packed light brown sugar
¹/₄ pound unsalted butter at room
    temperature
2 large eggs
2 teaspoons pure vanilla extract
1¹/₂ cups peanut M&M's

✴ Preheat oven to 350°F. In a sifter combine the flour, baking soda, and salt. Sift onto a large piece of waxed paper and set aside until needed.

✴ Heat 1 inch of water in the bottom of a double boiler over medium heat. With the heat on, place the semisweet chocolate in the top half of the double boiler. Use a rubber spatula to stir the chocolate until completely melted and smooth, about 4 to 5 minutes. Transfer to a small bowl and set aside.

✴ Place the granulated sugar, light brown sugar, and butter in a large bowl. Use a stiff rubber spatula (or wooden spoon) to cream the ingredients together until smooth. Add the eggs and vanilla extract and mix to incorporate. Add the melted chocolate and mix until combined. Add the dry sifted ingredients and thoroughly combine. Add the M&M's, mixing to incorporate.

✴ Using 3 heaping tablespoons of dough for each cookie, portion 6 cookies, evenly spaced, onto each of 3 nonstick baking sheets—or bake cookies in batches (this is a hefty cookie, so don't crowd). Place the baking sheets on the top and center racks of the preheated oven and bake for 14 minutes.

✴ Remove the cookies from the oven and cool to room temperature on the baking sheets, about 30 minutes. Store the cooled cookies in a tightly sealed plastic container until ready to serve.

Chocolate Decadence

NARSAI DAVID

1 pound semisweet chocolate
1¹/₄ sticks sweet butter
4 eggs
1 tablespoon sugar
1 tablespoon flour

Whipped Cream Frosting
1¹/₂ cups cream
1 teaspoon vanilla
1 tablespoon sugar

Raspberry Purée
One 10- to 12-ounce package frozen
  raspberries

SERVES 12

CHOCOLATE DECADENCE was developed AT NARSAI'S, AN award-winning RESTAURANT IN THE SAN FRANCISCO AREA FROM 1970 UNTIL 1986.

✳ Preheat oven to 425°F.

✳ Melt chocolate with butter in a double boiler until just melted. Pour into a bowl and set aside. Wash top of double boiler, place over water in bottom of double boiler and bring water back to a boil.

✳ Place eggs and sugar in top of double boiler and beat until sugar dissolves and mixture is lukewarm (do not overcook). Remove from heat and whip until about quadrupled in volume.

✳ Fold flour into eggs. Then stir one-fourth of egg mixture into chocolate and butter. Then fold entire chocolate and sugar mixture back into remaining egg mixture.

✳ Pour batter into an 8-inch cake pan that has been buttered, floured, and the bottom lined with parchment paper. Bake in preheated oven for 15 minutes, and no longer. (The cake will be liquid in the center.) Remove pan from oven, allow to cool, and freeze, preferably overnight, before removing from pan.

✳ Before removing dessert from freezer, make whipped cream and raspberry purée. Whip cream with vanilla and sugar until soft peaks develop. Defrost raspberries, purée in blender, and press through a fine sieve to remove seeds.

✳ To remove chocolate decadence from pan, carefully dip bottom of pan in hot water to unmold dessert. Top with whipped cream, masking any faults. Refrigerate until ready to serve.

✳ To serve, slice dessert into 12 pieces. Either drizzle 2 to 3 tablespoons of raspberry purée onto plate followed by a slice of chocolate decadence, or drizzle raspberry purée over a slice of chocolate decadence on the plate.

Italian Celebration Cake

TOM LACALAMITA

SERVES 8

ITALIANS, WHO ARE GENERALLY NOT BIG ON DESSERTS, WOULD MAKE THIS FOR A special OCCASION. THE LADY-FINGERS THAT CIRCLE THE cake CREATE A BEAUTIFUL FINISH.

Espresso Pastry Cream
2¹/₂ cups milk
¹/₂ cup espresso coffee beans, coarsely chopped
4 large eggs
4 large egg yolks
1 cup granulated sugar
4 tablespoons unbleached all-purpose flour

Sponge Cake
1 cup unbleached all-purpose flour
1 teaspoon baking powder
4 large eggs, separated, plus 1 whole large egg
²/₃ cup granulated sugar
Pinch of salt

2 tablespoons dark rum mixed with ¹/₄ cup water (optional)
1 package (3 ounces) soft ladyfingers
¹/₃ cup sliced almonds

✻ To prepare the pastry cream, bring the milk and coffee beans to a boil in a medium-size saucepan. Remove from heat, cover, and let sit 10 minutes. Pour into a second saucepan through a fine-mesh strainer. Discard the coffee beans.

✻ In a large mixing bowl, beat together the whole eggs, yolks, sugar, and flour until well combined. Bring the coffee-flavored milk to a boil. Lower the heat and gradually whisk in the egg mixture. Stir constantly until the pastry cream begins to thicken and comes to a boil. Remove from heat and pour the cream into a nonreactive bowl. Cover with a piece of plastic wrap, pushing the plastic into the custard so that a skin does not form. Let cool.

✻ To prepare the sponge cake, preheat the oven to 375°F. Butter and flour a 9-inch round cake pan. Sift the flour and baking powder into a large mixing bowl. Set aside.

✻ Beat the egg yolks, whole egg, and ⅓ cup of the sugar in a large mixing bowl until the mixture is thick and lemon-colored. Fold in the flour mixture. Set the batter aside.

✻ In a large bowl, beat the egg whites with salt until stiff peaks form. Gradually add the remaining ⅓ cup sugar and beat until glossy. Fold one-third of the batter into the beaten egg whites, until incorporated. Repeat process two more times. Pour the batter into the prepared pan and bake until the cake is golden and springs back when pressed, 20 to 25 minutes. Let cool 10 minutes, then remove the cake to a wire rack to cool completely.

✻ To assemble the dessert, cut cake in half horizontally once it has cooled. Place one half, cut side up, on a large serving plate. Sprinkle, if desired, with half of the diluted rum, then spread with one-third of the pastry cream. Place the second layer of cake, cut side down, on top of the first. Sprinkle, if desired, with the remaining diluted rum, then spread with half of the remaining pastry cream. Gently break the ladyfingers in half, lengthwise. Attach them around the perimeter of the cake, broken side down, by spreading them with the remaining pastry cream. Cover the top of the cake with sliced almonds.

Banana Layer Cake with Peanut Butter Buttercream

WAYNE BRACHMAN

SERVES 8 TO 12

WAYNE BRACHMAN

CREATED THIS LAYER CAKE

TO EMULATE THE

dramatic STRATIFIED

ROCK FORMATIONS

FOUND IN THE SOUTH-

WEST. THIS LAYER cake

HAS STRATA OF BANANA

CAKE AND PEANUT

BUTTER FROSTING THAT

RUN VERTICALLY INSTEAD

OF HORIZONTALLY. Plan

ON STARTING THIS CAKE

A day AHEAD; THE CAKE

LAYERS NEED TO SET IN

THE freezer FOR AT

LEAST 4 HOURS.

Banana Cake
2 1/2 cups cake flour
1 teaspoon baking soda
1/4 teaspoon baking powder
1/4 teaspoon salt
12 tablespoons unsalted butter,
    at room temperature
1 1/4 cups sugar
3 large eggs, at room temperature
3 large very ripe bananas
1/2 cup sour cream
1 tablespoon vanilla extract

Peanut Butter Buttercream
16 tablespoons (1/2 cup) unsalted butter,
    at room temperature
1 (18-ounce) jar creamy peanut butter
2 1/2 cups confectioners' sugar

Decorations
1/2 cup whole unsalted peanuts, plus
    1/2 cup chopped unsalted peanuts
1 ounce semisweet chocolate, melted

✳ To make the cake, set a rack in the middle of the oven and preheat to 375°F. Lightly grease the sides of two 15½- x 10-inch jelly-roll pans. Line them with parchment or buttered wax paper.

✳ Sift the flour, baking soda, baking powder, and salt together onto a sheet of waxed paper. Sift two more times to mix and aerate.

✳ Put the butter and sugar in the bowl of an electric mixer and beat at high speed for 30 seconds, or until well combined and smooth. Add the eggs one at a time, beating until each is incorporated. Continue beating, scraping down the sides of the bowl if necessary, until the mixture is light and fluffy and doubled in volume, approximately 5 more minutes.

✳ In a small bowl, using the mixer or a fork, mash the bananas until soupy. Stir in the sour cream and vanilla.

✳ With the mixer on its lowest setting, or using a rubber spatula, beat or fold one-third of the flour mixture into the butter mixture. Beat or fold in half of the banana mixture, then another third of the flour mixture. Beat or fold in the remaining banana mixture and then the remaining flour mixture.

✳ Divide the batter between the prepared pans, spreading it evenly with an offset metal spatula. Bake for 15 minutes, or until just golden and the centers spring back when lightly pressed. Cool the cakes in the pan on wire racks.

✳ To make the buttercream, put the butter and peanut butter in the bowl of an electric mixer and beat at medium speed until blended. Reduce the speed to low and gradually beat in the sugar. Increase the speed to medium and beat for 3 minutes, or until smooth and fluffy.

✳ To assemble the cake, cover each cake with a sheet of waxed paper or parchment paper. Place a large baking sheet over one cake, and carefully flip the cake over. Peel off the parchment. With a serrated knife or a pizza wheel, trim the edges of the cake. Using a ruler as a guide, cut ten 2- x 15-inch strips from the cake. Repeat with the second cake. Reserve one-third of the buttercream, and spread the remaining buttercream evenly over the cake strips.

✳ Disassemble a 9-inch springform pan, and wrap the bottom in plastic wrap. Tightly roll one cake strip up like a jelly roll, and stand it on end in the center of the pan bottom. Coil the remaining strips around the first, butting the ends together to form one large spiral. Fit the side pieces of the springform on and snap it closed. Freeze for at least 4 hours, or overnight.

✳ Just before serving, make the decorations. Arrange the whole peanuts in little clusters on a plate covered with waxed paper. Melt the chocolate in a small bowl set over a saucepan of barely simmering water. Using a fork, drizzle the chocolate over the peanuts. Refrigerate for 15 minutes to set.

✳ Soak a towel in hot water and squeeze dry. Wrap it around the springform pan to loosen the sides. Remove the sides of the pan and invert the cake onto a serving platter or cardboard cake round. Using a metal spatula, frost the top and sides of the cake with the reserved buttercream. Press the chopped peanuts into the sides of the cake, and decorate the top with the chocolate-covered peanut clusters. Serve at room temperature. The cake can be covered and stored in the refrigerator for up to 3 days.

Tunnel of Fudge Cheesecake

SHARON TYLER HERBST

Cookies 'n' Cream Crust

1 1/2 cups Oreo or Hydrox cookie crumbs
   (approximately 22 cookies), including
   the filling
3 tablespoons unsalted butter, melted

5 (8-ounce) packages cream cheese,
   softened
1 1/2 cups sugar

5 eggs
1/4 cup all-purpose flour
1/2 teaspoon salt
1/4 cup whipping cream
3 ounces semisweet chocolate, melted and
   cooled
1/2 cup semisweet chocolate chips
1 tablespoon pure vanilla extract
Sweetened whipped cream

✷ To make the cookies 'n' cream crust, preheat the oven to 350°F. Lightly grease a 9-inch springform pie pan. In a medium bowl, stir together the cookie crumbs and butter. Turn the mixture into the prepared pan with the back of a large spoon, pressing firmly and evenly over the bottom and up the sides of the pan. Bake for 10 minutes; remove and let cool to room temperature. Raise the heat to 400°F.

✷ In a large bowl, beat the cream cheese and sugar together until smooth and fluffy. Add the eggs, one at a time, beating after each addition. Beat in the flour, salt, and cream.

✷ Place 2 cups of the cheese mixture in a medium bowl. Stirring constantly, gradually add the melted chocolate, blending until well combined. Stir in the chocolate chips; set aside. Stir the vanilla into the remaining cheese mixture.

✷ Pour all but 1½ cups of the light cheese mixture into the prepared crust. Spoon the chocolate-cheese filling in a 2-inch-wide ring onto the light cheese mixture, 1½ inches from the edge of the pan. Do not get any in the center of the light mixture. Using the back of a spoon, press the chocolate mixture down into the light mixture until the top is level. Spoon the reserved light cheese mixture evenly over all and smooth the top.

✷ Place the cheesecake in the center of the middle oven rack. Position a 13- x 9-inch baking pan filled halfway with hot water on a lower shelf. Bake for 15 minutes. Reduce the heat to 300°F; bake an additional 50 minutes.

✷ Turn the oven off. Let the cheesecake cool in the oven for 1 hour with the oven door open 1 to 3 inches. Remove cheesecake from the oven to a rack; let cool completely. Cover and refrigerate overnight.

✷ To serve, run a thin knife around the inside edge of the pan; remove the side of the pan. Use a thin knife to loosen the crust from the bottom of the pan. With two large metal spatulas, carefully slide the cheesecake off the pan bottom and onto a serving plate. Spread the whipped cream over the top. Chill for at least 1 hour before serving.

SERVES 10 TO 12

IT WAS MAE WEST WHO SAID, "TOO MUCH OF A GOOD THING CAN BE wonderful," AND SHARON TYLER HERBST, WHO DUG UP THE QUOTATION, ALSO CREATED THIS show-stopper DESSERT, WHICH GETS TOP VOTES FROM HER STUDENTS. THIS cheesecake NEEDS TO BE MADE A DAY BEFORE SERVING. AVOID USING DOUBLE-STUFFED Oreo COOKIES FOR THE CRUST.

SERVES 10 TO 16

BESTSELLING COOKBOOK

AUTHOR LORA BRODY'S

family HAS MADE THIS

THEIR FAVORITE DESSERT

FOR birthdays AND

SPECIAL OCCASIONS.

Heavenly Chocolate Roll

LORA BRODY

Cake
8 extra-large eggs, separated and at room
 temperature
1¼ cups granulated sugar
Scant ⅓ cup cocoa (not Dutch process),
 plus extra for garnish
Scant ⅓ cup all-purpose flour, sifted

Filling
2 pints premium ice cream, softened

Topping
Hot Fudge Sauce (see page 171)
Whipped cream

✻ Preheat oven to 350°F.

✻ In a stand mixer with a paddle blade, beat the egg yolks until frothy. Turn mixer to high, add ½ cup of the sugar, and beat until the mixture is very thick and light yellow in color.

✻ Shift speed on mixer to low and add cocoa and flour. Blend only until ingredients are incorporated (do not overbeat). In a separate bowl, beat the egg whites with the remaining sugar until stiff, but not dry, as for a soufflé. Carefully fold the egg whites into the cocoa mixture.

✻ Pour the cocoa mixture into a 10 x 15-inch jelly roll pan that has been greased, lined with parchment paper, and greased again. Spread the mixture evenly with a spatula.

✻ Bake for 15 to 17 minutes, or until the edges just begin to pull away from the sides of the pan. Set the pan on a rack and cover the top of the cake with a slightly damp kitchen towel and allow to cool at room temperature, at least 1 hour.

✻ Sift a layer of cocoa evenly over the top of the cake. Cover with 2 long overlapping strips of plastic wrap. Cover with another baking sheet and invert cake onto plastic wrap and baking sheet. Carefully peel off parchment paper.

✻ Spread the softened ice cream over the cake, leaving 1 inch of unfilled border around the edges. Using the plastic wrap underneath as a guide, roll the cake like a jelly roll and slide seam of roll onto a board or platter. (Rolling from the long side gives an elegant, slender roll that can be cut into 14 to 16 small slices. Rolling from the shorter side produces a shorter, fatter roll and bigger slices.) Wrap cake roll in the plastic wrap or aluminum foil. Freeze for several hours.

✻ To serve, cut slices, pour hot fudge sauce over the top, and finish with whipped cream.

Hot Fudge Sauce

LORA BRODY

8 ounces bittersweet chocolate, coarsely
   chopped
4 ounces unsweetened chocolate, coarsely
   chopped

3 tablespoons sweet butter, cut into small
   pieces
$1/2$ cup firmly packed brown sugar
2 cups heavy cream

✱ Place the chocolate, butter, and brown sugar in the work bowl of a food processor fitted with a plastic blade.

✱ Heat the cream in a 2-quart saucepan set over medium heat. As soon as bubbles appear around the edge of the pan, lower the heat and allow the cream to come to a boil. If the cream threatens to overflow the pan, lower the heat and stir vigorously with a wire whisk. Allow the cream to simmer for 15 minutes, stirring occasionally.

✱ With the processor off, pour the hot cream through the feed tube. Replace the plunger and process until smooth, about 20 seconds. This can also be done with a hand blender; be sure to use a deep bowl to avoid spattering.

✱ Use immediately over Heavenly Chocolate Roll (see recipe page 170) or store in a covered container in the refrigerator or freezer.

THIS HOT FUDGE SAUCE CAN BE MADE UP TO 2 WEEKS ahead. REFRIGERATE IN A COVERED CONTAINER AND warm IN THE MICROWAVE, OR FREEZE FOR up TO 6 MONTHS.

Dairy-Free Chocolate-Almond Cake

CLAIRE CRISCUOLO

SERVES 8 TO 12

A great-tasting

DESSERT WITH TOFU

AND SOY MILK? IT'S

POSSIBLE…AND HERE'S

AN EXAMPLE. TO dress

THE CAKE UP A BIT, USE

ICING OF YOUR CHOICE

AND FINISH WITH SLIVERED

almonds.

2¼ cups unbleached white flour
4 teaspoons baking powder
¼ teaspoon salt
1⅔ cups sugar
1 cup unsweetened cocoa

½ cup (1 stick) soybean margarine,
    softened to room temperature
⅔ cup soft tofu, crumbled and drained
1¼ cups soy milk
1 teaspoon pure almond extract
1 cup slivered almonds

✻ Preheat oven to 350°F. Measure the flour, baking powder, salt, sugar, and cocoa into a bowl.

✻ Measure the soy margarine, tofu, soy milk, and almond extract into a blender. Cover and blend on low speed for 5 seconds. Stop to scrape down sides using a rubber spatula. Cover again and blend on high speed for 1 minute, stopping once to scrape down the sides.

✻ Pour the blended ingredients over the dry ingredients all at once. Beat lightly with a wooden spoon for about 30 seconds to mix. Stir in almonds.

✻ Spray a 10-inch Bundt pan with nonstick cooking oil spray.

✻ Turn the batter into the prepared pan, using a rubber spatula to scrape the bowl. Spread the batter smooth.

✻ Bake for about 50 minutes, until a cake tester inserted into the center comes out clean. Remove the pan from the oven and let set for 2 minutes before turning onto a cake dish.

Orange-Pistachio Torte with Ricotta and Fresh Fruit

MARLENE SOROSKY

Orange-Pistachio Cake
1 medium orange
1/3 cup plus 1/3 cup sugar
2 cups shelled, unsalted pistachio nuts, chopped (approximately 10 1/2 ounces)
1/2 cup plus 1 tablespoon all-purpose flour
3/4 teaspoon baking powder
1/8 teaspoon salt
9 large eggs, separated
3/4 cup orange marmalade
1 1/2 teaspoons vanilla extract

Ricotta Filling
2 cups whole-milk or part-skim ricotta cheese (approximately 1 pound)
1/4 cup frozen orange juice concentrate, thawed
1/3 cup confectioners' sugar
Assorted fresh fruits, such as oranges, berries, sliced kiwi, sliced plums, sliced nectarines, red and green grapes, and sliced papaya

✱ To make the cake, preheat the oven to 350°F. Lightly grease two 8 1/2- or 9-inch layer-cake pans. Cut a circle of parchment or wax paper to fit the bottoms and grease the paper.

✱ Using a sharp vegetable peeler, peel the orange zest, cutting off any white pith, which may be bitter. Reserve the fruit for the filling. Place the zest in a food processor with the metal blade. Add 1/3 cup sugar and process until finely ground, scraping the bottom and sides often. Add the nuts and pulse until finely ground. Pulse in the flour, baking powder, and salt.

✱ In a large mixing bowl, beat the egg yolks with 1/3 cup sugar until very thick and light, approximately 3 to 5 minutes. Mix in the marmalade and vanilla. On low speed, mix in the nut mixture just until incorporated.

✱ In a small mixing bowl with clean beaters, beat the egg whites until stiff-but-moist peaks form. Partially fold a third of the whites into the nut mixture and then fold in the remainder. Divide the batter between the prepared pans. Bake for 25 to 30 minutes, or until a toothpick inserted in the center comes out clean. Remove to racks and let cool for 20 minutes. Run a sharp knife around the sides and let cool for 30 minutes more. Invert onto racks to cool completely. (Cakes may be wrapped in foil and stored at room temperature overnight or frozen.)

✱ To make the filling, drain off any excess liquid from the ricotta. In a mixing bowl with an electric mixer, beat the ricotta until thick and light, approximately 2 minutes. Mix in the orange juice concentrate and confectioners' sugar.

✴ To assemble (up to 8 hours before serving), cut each cake layer in half horizontally. This is easiest to do on a turntable, marking the cake with toothpicks and using a serrated knife. Place one cake layer cut-side up on the cake plate. Spread with ½ cup filling. Top with the second cake layer cut-side up and spread with ½ cup filling. Halve the orange and slice it ¼-inch thick. Arrange a thick layer of orange and other fruit filling. Top with a third cake layer, spread with ½ cup filling, and top with the final cake layer, cut-side down. Spread the top with the remaining filling and arrange the fruit attractively on top. Cover with plastic wrap and refrigerate for at least 1 hour. The torte may be refrigerated up to 8 hours.

Strawberries in a Sea of Mango

MARTHA ROSE SHULMAN

1 large mango, peeled and pitted
2 tablespoons fresh lime juice
1 tablespoon sugar

1 pint strawberries, hulled and quartered
Fresh mint leaves, for garnish

✴ Place the mango, 1 tablespoon lime juice, and 1 teaspoon sugar in a food processor fitted with the metal blade or in a blender and purée. You should have approximately 1 cup of purée.

✴ In a nonreactive bowl, toss the strawberries with the remaining lime juice and sugar and let sit for 15 to 30 minutes if possible to draw out their juices.

✴ To serve, spoon ¼ cup mango purée onto a dessert plate or bowl and top with strawberries. Garnish with mint and serve.

SERVES 4

THIS sensuous, BEAU-
TIFUL DESSERT, FROM
MARTHA ROSE SHULMAN,
ALWAYS GETS raves AT
HER DINNER PARTIES. THE
mango PURÉE CAN BE
MADE A DAY AHEAD OF
TIME AND STORED IN
THE REFRIGERATOR. THE
strawberries CAN
BE PREPARED A FEW
HOURS BEFORE SERVING.

Drunken Bananas
with Candied Spiced Almonds

SERVES 6

Candied Spiced Almonds

1 tablespoon, plus ¹/₂ teaspoon
   unsalted butter
2 tablespoons sugar
¹/₂ cup slivered almonds
1 pinch cayenne pepper
1 pinch ground cinnamon
1 pinch chili powder
1 squirt of lemon juice

Caramel Sauce

¹/₂ cup maple syrup or brown sugar
¹/₄ cup dark rum or bourbon
2 tablespoons unsalted butter
Pinch of salt
¹/₄ cup evaporated skim milk

6 bananas, sliced on a deep bias into
   2-inch chunks
Frozen vanilla yogurt or ice cream,
   for garnish (optional)

THIS LOW-FAT DESSERT HAS TREMENDOUS DEPTH OF flavor AND TEXTURE WITH ITS WARM, SOFT BANANAS, crunchy, SWEET NUTS, AND THE COOL FROZEN YOGURT. BE EXTREMELY careful WHEN WORKING WITH THE caramel SAUCE, WHICH SHOULD NEVER COME IN CONTACT WITH YOUR SKIN. ALSO BE SURE TO REMOVE THE PAN FROM THE heat BEFORE LIGHTING THE rum.

✳ To make the candied spiced almonds, place 1 tablespoon of the butter and the sugar in a small saucepan and cook over low heat, stirring constantly, until melted and golden brown.

✳ In a small bowl, toss the almonds with the cayenne, cinnamon, and chili powder. Add the spiced nuts to the melted sugar and cook over low heat, stirring constantly, until the nuts are golden brown, approximately 5 to 7 minutes. Remove from the heat, and stir in the remaining ½ teaspoon butter and lemon juice. Transfer the candied nuts to a plate and let cool.

✳ To make the caramel sauce, in a large skillet cook the maple syrup over medium heat until it has reduced in volume by half. (If using brown sugar, just heat it through before adding the rum or bourbon.) Pour in the rum, remove from the heat, and then ignite the sauce with a lighted match. (The flame should burn out after a few seconds.) Return the pan to the heat and continue to cook over medium heat until the sauce is reduced to a light caramel consistency.

✳ Remove the pan from the heat. Add the butter, salt, and milk and stir until fully incorporated and smooth. Set aside.

✳ Lightly grease the bananas with vegetable spray or melted butter. Place a sauté pan over high heat until it is very hot. Add the bananas and sauté over medium heat until golden and tender, approximately 2 to 3 minutes on each side.

✳ To serve, scoop some frozen yogurt or ice cream, if desired, onto the center of each plate. Arrange the bananas around the yogurt and drizzle the caramel sauce around the entire plate. Garnish with the candied spiced almonds.

Frontera Grill's Chocolate Pecan Pie

RICK BAYLESS

Crust

1 1/2 cups all-purpose flour

6 tablespoons chilled unsalted butter,
   cut into 1/2-inch bits

3 tablespoons vegetable shortening,
   cut into 1/2-inch bits

3/4 teaspoon sugar

1/4 teaspoon salt

Ice water

1 egg yolk, beaten slightly

Filling

2 cups pecan halves (make sure they're
   fresh and flavorful)

6 ounces semisweet or bittersweet
   chocolate

3 tablespoons all-purpose flour

3/4 cup (1 1/2 sticks) room-temperature
   unsalted butter

1 cup firmly packed dark brown sugar

5 large eggs, at room temperature

3/4 cup light corn syrup

1/4 cup molasses

1 1/2 tablespoons Kahlúa or brandy

2 1/4 teaspoons pure vanilla extract

1/2 teaspoon salt

2 cups Sweetened Whip Cream (*see page
   179*) for serving

✳ To make the crust, measure the flour, butter, and shortening into a bowl or a food processor fitted with a metal blade. Quickly work the fats into the flour with a pastry blender or pulse the food processor until the flour looks a little damp (not powdery), but tiny bits of fat are visible. If using a food processor, transfer the mixture to a bowl.

✳ Mix together the sugar, salt, and 3 tablespoons of ice water in a small bowl. Using a fork, little by little work the ice-water mixture into the flour mixture. The dough will be in rough, rather stiff clumps; if there is unincorporated flour in the bottom of the bowl, sprinkle in a little more ice water and use the fork to work it together. Press the dough together into a flat disk, wrap in plastic, and refrigerate at least 1 hour.

✳ On a lightly floured surface, roll the dough into a 12-inch circle. Transfer to a deep 10-inch glass pie pan (Rick Bayless suggests rolling the dough onto the rolling pin, then unrolling it onto the pie pan). Decoratively crimp the edge and trim excess dough. Refrigerate 30 minutes.

✳ To prebake the crust, preheat the oven to 400°F. Lightly oil a 15-inch piece of foil and lay it, oiled side down, into the crust (heavy-duty aluminum foil is too stiff to work here);

press down to line the crust snugly. Fill with beans or pie weights and bake about 15 minutes, until beginning to brown around the edges. Reduce the oven temperature to 350°F. Carefully remove the beans (or weights) and foil, return the crust to the oven, and bake 8 to 10 minutes, until it no longer looks moist. (If crust bubbles at this point, gently press it down with the back of a spoon.) Brush the beaten egg yolk over the crust, then let cool completely.

✳ While the crust is cooling, spread the pecans on a baking sheet and toast in a 350°F oven until fragrant, about 10 minutes. Cool, then break into small pieces and transfer to a large bowl. Chop the chocolate into rough, ½-inch pieces and add to bowl, along with the flour. Stir until everything is well coated.

✳ To make the filling, cream the butter and brown sugar in a food processor (or in a large bowl of a stand mixer) until light and fluffy, about 3 minutes in the food processor, 5 minutes in the mixer. With the machine still running, add the eggs 1 at a time, letting each be completely incorporated before adding the next. Beat in the corn syrup, molasses, Kahlúa or brandy, vanilla, and salt.

✳ To bake the pie, pour the filling over the chocolate and pecans and stir well to combine. Pour the mixture into the prebaked pie shell, set onto the lower rack of the oven, and bake until a knife inserted into the center is withdrawn clean, about 1 hour.

✳ Cool pie completely on a wire rack. Serve slices of the pie at room temperature or slightly warm, topped with a dollop of Kahlúa-spiked, Sweetened Whip Cream.

Sweetened Whip Cream

1 cup heavy cream
1 tablespoon powdered sugar

1 teaspoon vanilla extract
1 tablespoon Kahlúa

✳ With either a stand mixer or by hand, whip cream until it holds a luscious, soft peak, then whip in sugar, vanilla extract, and Kahlúa. *Makes 2 cups.*

S'more Pie

SHARON TYLER HERBST

Crust
1 1/2 cups graham cracker crumbs
6 tablespoons unsalted butter, melted

Filling
1 1/2 cups whipping cream
12 ounces semisweet or milk chocolate, finely chopped
2 teaspoons pure vanilla extract
2 (7-ounce) jars marshmallow creme

SERVES 8 TO 10

THIS delicious AND EASY PIE WILL BRING BACK CHILDHOOD MEMORIES OF campfire S'MORES. SHARON TYLER HERBST CREATED THIS PIE AT THE REQUEST OF HER 12-YEAR-OLD NEPHEW. YOU CAN shortcut THIS RECIPE BY USING A STORE-BOUGHT CRUST. SERVE WITH FRESH berries, IF DESIRED.

✻ To prepare the crust, preheat the oven to 350°F and butter a 9-inch pie pan. In a medium bowl, combine the graham cracker crumbs and the melted butter and turn them into the pie pan. Use the back of a large spoon to press the mixture firmly and evenly over the bottom and up the sides of the pan. Bake for 10 minutes. Cool completely before filling.

✻ To prepare the filling, in a 4-cup glass measuring cup, combine the cream and chocolate. Microwave on High for 1 1/2 minutes; stir well. Microwave 1 more minute; stir until the mixture is smooth and creamy. (The mixture may require an additional 30 seconds of heating, depending on the microwave wattage.) Alternatively, combine the cream and chocolate in a medium saucepan. Heat over medium-low heat, stirring often, until the chocolate is melted and the mixture is smooth. For either method, stir the vanilla into the melted chocolate mixture, blending well. Pour into the cooled crust and refrigerate for at least 4 hours.

✻ Position the rack 4 inches from the broiling unit and preheat the broiler. Spoon dollops of marshmallow creme over the surface of the pie. Gently spread over the surface, leaving a 1-inch border around the edges of the crust (the marshmallow will spread when heated). If you're using a glass pie plate, place the pie in the middle of a 10- x 15-inch jelly-roll pan; surround the plate with ice cubes. (This will prevent the broiler heat from cracking the cold pie plate; it's not necessary to do this with a metal pan.) Broil the pie until the marshmallow surface is browned to your liking, turning the pan as necessary for even heat.

✻ Serve immediately or refrigerate until ready to serve. Use a serrated blade to decrease the possibility of the top's cracking when you cut through the thin layer of crisp toasted marshmallow.

Peachy Apple Cobbler

SERVES 6

YOU CAN vary THIS COBBLER BY SUBSTITUTING OTHER DRIED fruit FOR THE PEACHES, SUCH AS DRIED APRICOTS, BLUEBERRIES, OR cherries. IF YOU ARE CONCERNED ABOUT CHOLESTEROL, YOU CAN USE 3 EGGS AND 2 EGG WHITES IN PLACE OF THE 4 EGGS.

1 pound McIntosh or Winesap apples
1/2 cup dried peaches
4 eggs
3/4 cup sugar
2 teaspoons vanilla extract
1 tablespoon rum
1 cup all-purpose flour
1 1/2 cups milk, preferably low-fat or skim
Frozen vanilla yogurt and powdered sugar, for garnish (optional)

✴ Peel, quarter, and slice the apples into 1/8-inch-thick slices. Coarsely chop the peaches. Set aside.

✴ In an electric mixer, beat the eggs and sugar until fluffy. Add the vanilla and rum and beat again. Slowly add the flour until fully incorporated; then add the milk and beat until mixed well.

✴ Preheat the oven to 350°F. Lightly grease a 9- x 12-inch baking dish. Spread the apples and peaches evenly across the bottom of the dish. Pour the batter over the fruit.

✴ Bake for 40 to 45 minutes, or until the top of the cobbler is golden brown and a toothpick inserted in the center comes out clean. Serve warm with a scoop of frozen vanilla yogurt and powdered sugar, if desired.

Caramelized Apple Tarts

MARGARET CHISHOLM

Flaky Sweet Pastry

1 1/4 cups all-purpose flour

1/2 cup unsalted butter, chilled and
cut into small pieces

1 tablespoon sugar

Pinch of salt

3 tablespoons ice water

4 tart apples such as Golden Delicious or
Granny Smith

4 tablespoons unsalted butter

1/4 cup sugar

1 egg

Pinch of salt

1 tablespoon brown sugar (optional)

✳ To make the pastry, place the flour, butter, sugar, and salt in a food processor. Pulse 6 or 7 seconds, just until the mixture is the size of lima beans. With the machine running, add the ice water and pulse 3 or 4 times, just until the pastry begins to hold together. Do not let it form a ball.

✳ Remove the pastry from the machine. Place on a floured surface and shape into four small disks approximately 3 inches in diameter and 1/2-inch thick. Refrigerate for at least 1 hour or up to 2 days.

✳ Preheat the oven to 425°F.

✳ Peel and core the apples. Cut each into 12 even wedges.

✳ In a large skillet, melt the butter over medium-high heat. When it is hot but not quite smoking, add the apples, sprinkle with the sugar, and sauté until golden brown, approximately 10 minutes. Set aside to cool.

✳ Roll the dough into 7-inch circles, place the circles on an ungreased baking sheet, and set in the refrigerator for 10 minutes.

✳ In a small cup, whisk the egg with a pinch of salt.

✳ Place the apples in the center of each pastry circle in a circular pattern, leaving a 1-inch border around the edges. Fold the edges inward, making a fluted pattern. Brush the tops of the pastry with the beaten egg.

✳ Bake the tarts for approximately 20 minutes, or until golden on top. Sprinkle with brown sugar, if desired. Serve warm or at room temperature.

SERVES 4

THESE APPLE tarts, A RECIPE FROM VANCOUVER'S MARGARET CHISHOLM, ARE MADE free-standing, WITHOUT A TART PAN. THEY'RE NOT DIFFICULT TO MAKE AND THE caramelizing OF THE APPLES GIVES THEM A WONDERFUL FLAVOR. THE INDIVIDUAL PORTIONS MAKE THEM A festive ENDING FOR YOUR NEXT HOME-COOKED DINNER PARTY.

PERMISSIONS

From *Smoothies* by Mary Corpening Barber, Sara Corpening, and Lori Lyn Narlock (Chronicle Books, 1997) © 1997 by Mary Corpening Barber, Sara Corpening, and Lori Lyn Narlock: Banana Latte Smoothie, Classico Smoothie

From *Rick Bayless's Mexican Kitchen* by Rick Bayless (Scribner, 1996) © 1996 by Richard Lane Bayless: Rustic Ranch-Style Soup with Tomato, Jalapeño, and Avocado; Grilled Steak with Spicy Guajillo Sauce; Frontera Grill's Chocolate Pecan Pie

From *Cakes and Cowpokes* by Wayne Harley Brachman (William Morrow and Company, Inc., 1995) © 1995 by Wayne Harley Brachman: Banana Layer Cake with Peanut Butter Buttercream

From *The Foods and Flavors of Haute Provence* by Georgeanne Brennan (Chronicle Books, 1997) © 1997 by Georgeanne Brennan: Cabbage Salad with Prosciutto, Beef Daube with Dried Cèpes

From *Potager* by Georgeanne Brennan (Chronicle Books, 1992) © 1992 by Georgeanne Brennan: Savory Bread Pudding Layered with Asparagus, Fontina, and Mixed Herbs

From *The Kitchen Survival Guide* by Lora Brody (William Morrow and Company, Inc., 1992) © 1992 by Lora Brody: Caramelized Onion Soup, Ivy's Cranberry-Orange Turkey Breast

From *Pizza, Focaccia, Filled & Flat Breads from Your Bread Machine* by Lora Brody (William Morrow and Company, Inc., 1995) © 1995 by Lora Brody: Sourdough Pizza with Potatoes and Caramelized Onions

From *Flavored Oils: 50 Recipes for Cooking with Infused Oils* by Michael Chiarello, with Penelope Wisner (Chronicle Books, 1995) © 1995 by Michael Chiarello: Pasta with Tomato Vinaigrette; Pork Tenderloin with Molasses, Bacon, and Porcini Vinaigrette

From *Flavored Vinegars: 50 Recipes for Cooking with Infused Vinegars* by Michael Chiarello, with Penelope Wisner (Chronicle Books, 1996) © 1996 by Michael Chiarello: Grilled Mozzarella with Tomato Vinegar, Crazy Berries

From *Cookwise* by Shirley Corriher (William Morrow and Company, Inc.,1997) © 1997 by Shirley O. Corriher: Touch of Grace Biscuits

From *Claire's Classic Vegetarian Cooking* by Claire Criscuolo (Dutton, 1997) © 1997 by Claire Criscuolo: Tuscan Salad of Chicory, White Beans, and Hearts of Palm

From *Claire's Corner Copia Cookbook* by Claire Criscuolo (Viking, 1997) © 1997 by Claire Criscuolo: Dairy-Free Chocolate Almond Cake

From *Death by Chocolate Cookies* by Marcel Desaulniers (Simon & Schuster, 1997) © 1997 by Marcel Desaulniers: Deep-Dish Pizza Cookies, Road Trip Cookies

From *Salad Days* by Marcel Desaulniers (Simon & Schuster, 1998) © 1998 by Marcel Desaulniers: Roasted Root Vegetable Slaw with Gingered Apples, Raisins, Walnuts, and Barley

From *Fresh from the Farmers' Market* by Janet Fletcher (Chronicle Books, 1997) © 1997 by Janet Fletcher: Bruschetta with Sweet Peppers and Ricotta, Spaghettini with Red and Gold Cherry Tomatoes, Green Bean Salad with Cherry Tomatoes and Ricotta Salata

From *Recipes 1-2-3* by Rozanne Gold (Viking, 1996) © 1996 by Rozanne Gold: Black Olive Tapenade, Cornish Hen Under a Brick

From *The Food Lover's Guide to Chocolate and Vanilla* by Sharon Tyler Herbst (William Morrow and Company, Inc., 1996) © 1996 by Sharon Tyler Herbst: S'more Pie, Tunnel of Fudge Cheesecake

From *Party Food* by Barbara Kafka (William Morrow and Company, Inc., 1992) © 1992 by Barbara Kafka: Beef Empanadas

From *Roasting* by Barbara Kafka (William Morrow and Company, Inc., 1995) © 1995 by Barbara Kafka: Roasted Red Pepper Spread, Soothing Summer Turkey Salad

From *The Greek Vegetarian* by Diane Kochilas (St. Martin's Press, 1996) © 1996 by Diane Kochilas: Villager's Leek and Fennel Pie, Eggplant Stuffed with Onions and Kefalotiri

From *Espresso Desserts* by Tom Lacalamita (Simon & Schuster, 1995) © 1995 by Thomas N. Lacalamita: Italian Celebration Cake

From *The Ultimate Pressure Cooker Cookbook* by Tom Lacalamita (Simon & Schuster, 1997) © 1997 by Thomas N. Lacalamita: Home-Style Stuffed Artichokes, Chicken with Yogurt and Beer, Braised Farmhouse Chicken

From *How to Bake* by Nick Malgieri (HarperCollins, 1995) © 1995 by Nick Malgieri: Neapolitan Ricotta, Mozzarella, and Prosciutto Pie

From *James McNair's Burgers* by James McNair (Chronicle Books, 1992) © 1992 by James McNair: Knecht Burgers, New California Patty Melts, Three Nut Turkey Burgers

From *James McNair Cooks Italian* by James McNair (Chronicle Books, 1994) © 1994 by James McNair: Baked Dumplings, Roman Style, Chicken Cutlets with Prosciutto and Sage

From *James McNair's Grains and Beans* by James McNair (Chronicle Books, 1997) © 1997 by James McNair: Roasted Garlic and Bean Spread with Crusty Bread

From *James McNair's Vegetarian Pizza* by James McNair (Chronicle Books, 1993) © 1993 by James McNair: Salad Pizza, Olive Paste Pizza, Banana Satay Pizza

From *Pizza* by James McNair (Chronicle Books, 1987) © 1987 by James McNair: Basic Pizza Dough, Mozzarella and Tomato Pizza, Pizza with Garlic-Glazed Chicken

From *Joy of Cooking* by Irma S. Rombauer, Marion Rombauer Becker, and Ethan Becker (Scribner, 1997) © 1997 by Simon and Schuster, The Joy of Cooking Trust, and the MRB Revocable Trust: New Orleans Bread Pudding with Southern Whiskey Sauce, Chicken Jambalaya

From *Sauces* by Michel Roux (Rizzoli, 1996) © 1996 by Michel Roux: Yogurt Sauce

From *License to Grill* by Chris Schlesinger and John Willoughby (William Morrow and Company, Inc., 1997) © 1997 by Christopher Schlesinger and John Willoughby: Latin-Flavored Coleslaw with Grilled Avocados, Orange–Sweet Potato Pack, Grilled West Indies Spice-Rubbed Chicken Breast with Grilled Banana

From *Mexican Light* by Martha Rose Shulman (Bantam Books, 1996) © 1996 by Martha Rose Shulman: Black Bean Nachos; Basic Cheese Quesadillas Several Ways; Quesadillas with Goat Cheese, Roasted Peppers, and Black Beans; Strawberries in a Sea of Mango; Stewed Chicken with Chipotles and Prunes

From *Entertaining on the Run* by Marlene Sorosky (William Morrow and Company, Inc., 1994) © 1994 by Marlene Sorosky: Dried Apricot, Ham, and Leek-Stuffed Chicken Breasts; Orange-Pistachio Torte with Ricotta and Fresh Fruit

From *Good n' Healthy!* by Brenda C. Ward and Jane Cabiness Jarrel (Tommy Nelson, a division of Nelson-Word Publishing Group, 1995) © 1995 by Brenda C. Ward and Jane Cabiness Jarrel: Breakfast Pizza

From *New World Noodles* by Steven Wong (Robert Rose, Inc., 1997) © 1997 by Steven Wong and Bill Jones: Shredded Chicken Salad with Spicy Sesame Vinaigrette, Peppered Beef with Flat Rice Noodles, Satay-Glazed Vegetables with Cilantro Parmesan Noodles

From *The Great American Chocolate Contest Cookbook* by T. K. Woods (William Morrow and Company, Inc., 1995) © 1995 by Sparkatects, Inc.: Dee-Luxe Layered Choco-Oat Bars

The following recipes are courtesy of

Denis Blais:
Smoked Salmon Napoleons, Monterey Stuffed Chicken Breasts

Margaret Chisholm:
Cedar-Planked Salmon, Caramelized Apple Tarts

Narsai David:
Australian Flax and Sesame Seed Bread, Narsai's Assyrian Chicken, Chocolate Decadence

Soren C. Fakstorp:
Pan-Seared Salmon with Orange-Basil Pesto

Chris Johnson:
Grilled Ratatouille, Grilled Caesar Salad, Grilled Quail

Michael Noble:
Vegetable and Chorizo Frittata with Tomato-Basil Chutney, Whole Wheat Pancakes with Blueberry Compote

INDEX

TABLE OF EQUIVALENTS

The exact equivalents in the following tables have been rounded for convenience.

Liquid and Dry Measures

U.S.	METRIC
¼ teaspoon	1.25 milliliters
½ teaspoon	2.5 milliliters
1 teaspoon	5 milliliters
1 tablespoon (3 teaspoons)	15 milliliters
1 fluid ounce (2 tablespoons)	30 milliliters
¼ cup	60 milliliters
⅓ cup	80 milliliters
1 cup	240 milliliters
1 pint (2 cups)	480 milliliters
1 quart (4 cups, 32 ounces)	960 milliliters
1 gallon (4 quarts)	3.84 liters
1 ounce (by weight)	28 grams
1 pound	454 grams
2.2 pounds	1 kilogram

Length Measures

U.S.	METRIC
⅛ inch	3 millimeters
¼ inch	6 millimeters
½ inch	12 millimeters
1 inch	2.5 centimeters

Oven Temperatures

FAHRENHEIT	CELSIUS	GAS
250	120	½
275	140	1
300	150	2
325	160	3
350	180	4
375	190	5
400	200	6
425	220	7
450	230	8
475	240	9
500	260	10